John Tavener was born in North London in 1944. He demonstrated at an early age an exceptional gift for the piano and the organ. He none the less opted, at the age of twelve, for a life devoted to composing. His prolific output includes large-scale choral and orchestral works, dramatic works, liturgical settings, pieces in concertante form, short choral works, song cycles and string quartets. He has written more unaccompanied choral music than any composer since the Renaissance. He converted to the Orthodox faith in 1977.

John Tavener lives with his wife Maryanna and their two daughters on the Greek island of Evia, and also has a house in Sussex.

Brian Keeble is the founder of Golgonooza Press, and editor of the work of, amongst others, Cecil Collins, Philip Sherrard and Kathleen Raine. His *Art: For Whom and For What?* was published in 1998. He has enjoyed many years of close friendship with John Tavener, and much of their lives and cultural interests have run a parallel course.

The Music of Silence
A Composer's Testament

JOHN TAVENER

Edited by Brian Keeble

faber and faber
LONDON·NEW YORK

First published in 1999
by Faber and Faber Limited
3 Queen Square London WC1N 3AU
Published in the United States by Faber and Faber Inc.
a division of Farrar, Straus and Giroux, Inc., New York

Typeset by Faber and Faber Ltd
Printed in England by Clays Ltd, St Ives plc

A CIP record for this book
is available from the British Library

ISBN 0–571–20436–8 (limited edition)
0–571–20088–5 (pbk)

2 4 6 8 10 9 7 5 3 1

To Mother Thekla,
who has not only helped me spiritually,
but who has helped me put my
music and my life together

Contents

List of Illustrations

All photographs are from the Tavener family's private collection unless otherwise stated.

Acknowledgements

What book is ever made without the help of others? It is a pleasure for me to thank Maryanna Tavener, the composer's wife, for her generous hospitality and assistance in many practical matters. Philip Pilkington took pains to review our text at short notice and saved us from many errors. We are deeply grateful to him. We must also thank Paul Lewis who generously volunteered to compile the discography. Finally I would like to thank John Tavener for his invitation to undertake the task – a journey of discovery for us both.

The passage from C. S. Lewis's *The Magician's Nephew* that appears on p. 159 is reproduced by kind permission of Harper-Collins Publishers Ltd.

B.K.

A NOTE BY JOHN TAVENER

I would like to pay a debt of gratitude to my wife, Maryanna, who not only cares for me but who also enables me to go on writing (often when I am quite unwell).

Also to Archimandrite Vasileios of Iveron Monastery on Mount Athos. His writings are a constant inspiration to me, helping me to put my thoughts in order.

John Tavener
Evia, Greece

Prelude

It began with a telephone call from John Tavener one day in August 1998. A publisher was interested in a book of conversations – would I conduct them with him? A trip to Sussex and an afternoon's conversation with John convinced me that my hesitation was without foundation. After all, we had conducted many such conversations over the years. From this point onwards, and yet not altogether to my surprise, we discovered that the book took on a life of its own.

Two weeks later I received from John a dozen faxed pages of random, scribbled notes listing themes, works, people and events that might be grist to our dialogic mill. These notes formed the basis of two further four-day sessions, during which we mapped out the territory for a series of conversations. I then worked on the extensive notes compiled at these sessions with an eye to shaping them as my script for a series of recorded conversations which would not, so far as is possible without inhibiting spontaneity, duplicate or overlap material.

A review of the possible venues and their attendant hazards – at least in England – left us in no doubt that the best place to record was at John's home in Greece, with all communication channels severed. And so it was. Early in October, at Lefkandi, we recorded for about two and a half hours each morning for nine days – in all, about sixteen hours of conversation with only barking dogs and chickens to accompany us. The afternoons were for swimming in the sea and the evenings for the taverna. Towards the end of these sessions John decided to place a series of commentaries at the end of the conversations. Since these required reference to the relevant scores they were partly written and recorded back in Sussex early in the New Year. The transcripts of all the tapes became, in effect, our first draft of the Testament.

In December, we worked independently on this first draft, both cutting and transposing, John interpolating and augmenting. A further session together in Sussex in January saw our independent versions welded into a single text, which was sent to the publisher and to a long-standing friend of John's, whom we had recruited to play Devil's advocate. Their observations – challenges in many instances – led to one further session of exchange, argument and refinement.

We worked until the composer felt that the text had become his Testament. And so the task was done.

In Retrospect

ELEMENTAL SOUNDS

Music was the first thing I was aware of. I cannot remember a time when there was no music in my life. The earliest influence upon me was the sound of the elements. I hated sight-reading, or being taught any of the grammar of music. From the age of three, I used to improvise. We had little concerts, my maternal grandfather and I: he would pretend to be an audience, he would clap, and I remember I made the sound of rain, the sound of wind, the sound of thunder – elemental sounds on the piano: God knows what they sounded like. So it was with improvisation that I started.

Then I was taught the piano. The idea of being taught never appealed to me very much, because I thought I could find out musical tunes with my ear. That has guided me throughout my life.

My paternal grandfather, who owned a building business, had a huge studio in Hampstead, and I used to think the Christmas tree there was as big as the one in Trafalgar Square. It was a very grand, wood-panelled studio in Hampstead, built to entertain important clients of his business. I am not sure of the reason for putting the pipe organ in. He was musical; he liked the sound of the organ. Certainly at that period of my life I liked the sound of the organ. Nowadays, I cannot stand the sound of the monster. There was a piano, a double bass and my father's cello, my cousins brought along recorders and other instruments at Christmas, so we made a very merry noise. My father (who later carried on the family building business) played the cello and the organ, my paternal grandfather played the violin, my aunt played the piano, my uncle the double bass, and we used to sing and play together, with me playing on grandfather's pipe organ in the studio. I'll never forget those Christmases. They were enchanted.

I also remember when I was only three my mother was in hospital giving birth to my brother. My nanny told me that I listened endlessly to a 78 r.p.m. record which had the massed Manchester schoolchildren, conducted by Sir Hamilton Harty, singing on one side 'Nymphs and shepherds, come away' and on the other side 'Brother, come and dance with me' from *Hänsel and Gretel* by Humperdinck. I played it endlessly; it was almost a ritual. I had to hear it all the time. Maybe that was an expression of the fact that my mother was away and music was a great comfort to me.

This was my first introduction to the sound of a choir, and I can still, at the age of fifty-five, be moved by hearing that 78 r.p.m. record, but not because of the intrinsic quality of the music. What I love most of all is the sound of those massed children's voices with the inimitable accent of the fifties. This endless repetition of hearing a piece of music was important.

My mother's brother – and my father, for that matter – used to take me to the Albert Hall to hear Bach's *St Matthew Passion*. I shall never forget it. There was no applause, it was a very solemn Lenten occasion in those days. There were five hundred in the Bach Choir; Kathleen Ferrier was singing the contralto part and Peter Pears was the Evangelist, with Dr Reginald Jacques as the conductor. He used to sit, I seem to remember, to perform it. I shall never forget the opening sound, especially played by these large forces on non-period instruments. I think the very opening, just before the choir comes in, is one of the most beautiful sounds in all music. I remember thinking so at the time. And the effect of the *St Matthew Passion* was of a religious experience; it was all I knew of religion – just Bach.

I was also listening to Handel at this time, in the form of Thomas Beecham's orchestration of *Solomon*. Again, I listened to it entranced. I still do the same thing today but on period instruments. I go on listening and listening. I was, and still am, amazed by the sound of *Solomon*, the magic of the sound, the mystery of the sound. It's nothing intellectual: I don't think it ever has been intellectual with me. It was this mystery, and it was my ear that was picking up this wonderful music.

But by far the most powerful musical experience I had at this time was hearing Stravinsky's *Canticum Sacrum*. I heard the first broadcast performance from St Mark's, Venice, when I was twelve years old. That completely overwhelmed me, and made me really want to compose. For two or three years after it, I was imitating the sounds that I'd heard. It was an aural experience. I was just bowled over by the sound of it. Many years later I think I could explain why, but at the time I was shattered by its austerity.

I had heard things like the *The Rite of Spring*, *Petrushka* and *The Firebird*, of course. At that time I was collecting records and listening to a lot of Stravinsky. But none of it had the impact on me that this broadcast of *Canticum Sacrum* had. I subsequently managed to get hold of a very old Oiseau Lyre recording – the best performance I have ever heard – performed in acoustics similar to St Mark's, Venice. I think it needs to be performed in such an acoustic.

My knowledge of music during these years also came from concerts. I remember my parents taking me to Lucerne. I heard Karl Böhm conducting Beethoven symphonies; they didn't make a great impression on me. I heard Ernest Ansermet conducting Stravinsky, again in Switzerland, with L'Orchestre de la Suisse Romande. The Stravinsky pieces had a deep effect on me; I recall hearing in those days *Apollon Musagète*, the neoclassical Stravinsky. It was a curious mixture of Handel, Stravinsky and of course Bach.

Lady Birley, whom I came to think of as my godmother, took me for the very first time to Glyndebourne when I was twelve. In so many ways 1956 seems to me such a significant year. She looked like a wild gypsy; she was very beautiful. She had an Alvis car, I seem to recall she was swathed in scarves and we drove open-top

to Glyndebourne. These were the really great days of Glyndebourne when John and Audrey Christie were still there. The
effect of *The Magic Flute* on me was overwhelming. I had
already heard operas. I had even been to Covent Garden with
my father. I cannot recall what I heard there, but I thought it was
a stupid medium. But when I saw *The Magic Flute* I changed my
mind. I thought, this is a different matter, there does seem to be
a point to all those people up there apparently mucking about on
the stage. I think I recognized a sense of ritual, not only in *The
Magic Flute* but also in the *Canticum Sacrum*.

I think it was a *total* experience with *The Magic Flute*,
although perhaps primarily at that time it was musical. I sat there
completely riveted. It seemed to have so many levels to which one
could respond. It's not really an opera anyway: it's called a
Singspiel. It's a pantomime. They are not real characters; I like
that. At a later date I realized that the leading characters are
archetypes. It was very clear for a child or someone of twelve to
follow: you had a good man in Sarastro, you had the evil witch in
the Queen of the Night, you had a couple of fools in Papageno
and Papagena, and then you had the lovers in Tamino and Pamina, and you had a wicked old bugger in – a name I can never pro-
nounce – Monostatos, who lusts after Pamina.

At a much later date I discovered that all the symbolism in *The
Magic Flute* was masonic. I was disgusted at the time, because
Orthodoxy proscribes anything to do with freemasonry. How-
ever, this doesn't bother me any more.

Anyway, having no interest in opera, I suppose I went because
it was an experience. I would never go to Glyndebourne now
unless they decided to perform one of my works. But in those days
it was such a romantic thing to do and I had such a romantic godmother. We used to have amazing picnics, she used to park the
Alvis in a ditch and in the intervals we used to tuck into her unfor-
gettable pâté (she was a wonderful cook). There was something
special about the whole experience of going to Glyndbourne.

Only occasionally was my music-making in those early years

collaborative. Somewhat later, when I was at Highgate School, we got together a little group and had concerts in my grandfather's studio. Our group included the composer John Rutter, Nicholas Snowman who went on to found the London Sinfonietta and now runs Glyndebourne, and the pianist Francis Steiner. Simon Vaughan was the singer. We put on little concerts. For one of them I wrote, at about the age of fifteen (in 1959), what I consider to be the first of my important pieces. It was the first of what was to become the three *Donne Sonnets* and I seem to remember a performance of that with me playing the organ and Simon Vaughan singing the vocal part. It was a very severe text for somebody of fifteen to be attracted to:

> Spit in my face you Jewes, and pierce my side,
> Buffet, and scoffe, scourge, and crucifie mee,
> For I have sinn'd and sinn'd, and onely hee,
> Who could do no iniquitie hath dyed.

I never wanted to read music – I hated the idea. When I went to the local school of music it was something I detested – being taught, having to sight-read, all that aspect of music. Because I had perfect pitch, all I wanted to do was improvise. I never wanted to look at scores, I just wanted to listen. And improvise. And the organ is a very good instrument on which to improvise. Early on, in the Presbyterian church in Hampstead I listened to organists, or my own father, improvising before the service started. So I became an expert improviser, I might say, and I could improvise for hours at a time.

However, I did finally learn to read music, otherwise I wouldn't know how to write a score at all. But it was definitely the least interesting part of music. Music for me was something that I just did and I did it non-stop, as I still do today.

When I was aged about thirteen or fourteen, I wrote a *Duo Concertante* (1961) for trombone and piano for the headmaster of Highgate School. I remember he loved it, and played it, and he excused me from all games – football or 'fives' or whatever they played there. I was allowed to spend the entire afternoon in Highgate Parish Church improvising on the organ.

I didn't want to play Bach. By this time I could read music but I didn't really want to play Bach from the score, but rather from my memory of what I had heard. I remember listening and listening to the Sanctus from the *Mass in B Minor* and I got it absolutely right, because at a later date I checked it with the full score.

During the time I was at Highgate School it had a good reputation for being a musical school and its choir was second to none. It was Highgate School Choir who provided the boys' voices for the recording of the *War Requiem* conducted by Britten. The boys' voices were also used for a piece by Luigi Dallapiccola. There was an extraordinary man at the school, Edward Chapman, who could be extremely cruel. I recall him saying to a friend of mine who was trying to compose, 'You know, it costs a lot of money to buy manuscript paper . . . takes a long time to write it out . . . and you can't help wondering whether it's worth it.' He could be savage, absolutely savage.

I remember also that he thought my powers of extemporization were so good that he sent me up to Trinity College, Cambridge, at the age of fourteen to sit for an organ scholarship. Nobody at the age of fourteen could possibly do that. I'd never learnt anything about the laws of western counterpoint. I remember him coming into the school chapel the day before I went and he said, 'They'll probably ask you to transpose from a full score', and he put a full score in front of me and he said, 'Right, transpose that into C sharp.' Well, of course I couldn't do it – I'd never done it in my life! Then he said, 'They'll probably give you a paper on counterpoint. I know I haven't talked too much about it, but do it intuitively.' And I remember him telling me to play scales on the pedals, which he'd never ever gone through with me before. Of course, I was almost crying by the end of it – I thought, this is ridiculous, I won't be able to do anything. He said, 'But I think you may win through because of your power of extemporization.'

6

Well, I went up and I played for Raymond Leppard who was at Trinity at that time. I played the Bach Prelude and Fugue in B minor and I improvised. They were very impressed by my improvisation. As for the paper on counterpoint, I just filled it in with the notes that I felt sounded best. They actually wrote to Edward Chapman saying that I was extremely talented and ought to come up again in perhaps a couple of years' time.

My music had a curious mixture of influences at this time: Stravinsky, Gershwin, Ravel, Handel (rather more like the Percy Grainger Handel, *Handel in the Strand*, it had a kind of extra exuberance). Stravinsky was probably the strongest influence. I wrote pieces for the school orchestra, and Edward Chapman was very impressed with what I wrote. I was also quite a budding pianist. I played Shostakovich's Second Piano Concerto, as a duet, with Edward Chapman playing the orchestral part, at the Festival Hall while I was still at Highgate. I played Beethoven's Fourth Piano Concerto and Mozart's Piano Concerto No. 23 with the school orchestra. I also wrote lots of music for the orchestra. I cannot remember the titles of all the pieces, but it was a great experience for me because I could actually hear my music, and to hear was the most important thing for me.

There were annual carol services, and towards the end of my time at Highgate School Edward Chapman used to say, 'Right, get on the organ stall and play.' As I arrived at the carol service I thought I was going to sing in the choir as normal but he would say, 'Come over here. You play.' I said, 'I haven't got any music with me,' so he said, 'Improvise.' So I improvised. I've grown to hate the organ but in those days I absolutely loved playing it. I remember playing it extremely loudly. A hero of mine was Dr Thalben Ball who used to play Handel organ concertos in what many would now regard as the most outrageously philistine manner – as did Edward Chapman – with all the stops out and not remotely like the sound of a baroque organ. (I remember the first time I heard the word baroque, I must have been much younger. I was in St Albans Abbey and I was intrigued: they were building a new organ and I went up to – I suppose it must have been – the verger and I said, 'Is the organ baroque?' And he said, 'No, it's in perfectly good order.')

There were a lot of very musical people at Highgate when I was there. I have already mentioned the composer John Rutter, the pianist Francis Steiner and Nicholas Snowman; Howard Shelley, another good pianist, was also there, as was the composer Brian Chapple. So there were a lot of musical people there, under Edward Chapman's terrifying and inspiring tutelage.

I remember playing Bach's *Italian Concerto* in the big main hall. Edward Chapman sat there with his hands over his face. When I'd finished playing, he spoke to me about the great mystery of Bach's music, its spirituality. Despite his toughness, I was very lucky to have him, and in a way he was my best teacher, because he was already talking in almost metaphysical terms. He had a very naïve view of what would happen to him when he died: he believed that he would be playing the organ for the angels in heaven. He believed that totally. But he certainly conveyed to me, especially in the slow movement of the *Italian Concerto*, the mystery of Bach.

He also took me to the complete cycle of *The Ring* at Covent Garden, which intrigued me, I think – I can't say more than that. It intrigued, and somehow 'bothered' me.

Credo (1961) was composed while I was still at Highgate. I got a group of professional brass players together – my father, as always, footing the bill. Using the choir from my father's church, St Andrew's Presbyterian Church in Hampstead, *Credo* was given its first performance. Then I wrote a setting of *Genesis* (1962), the Creation of the World. I had interspersed into the biblical text verses from T. S. Eliot's 'The Rock'.

Even in those days I had considerable cheek, so I wrote to Eliot and invited him to come to this performance. Later, I read in the *Hampstead & Highgate Express*, 'T. S. Eliot will come to Tavener's Oratorio'. In the end he was unable to, he had a cold or something. I even sent him my poetry, the poetry I wrote when I was sixteen or seventeen, and he wrote a very kind letter back saying, 'Stick to your music, and as far as your poetry is concerned all I can say at the moment is that it is as good as anything I wrote when I was your age.'

As to other than musical influences, Stravinsky was such a hero in these early days, I tended to read what I'd seen Stravinsky had read. So it could be anything from T. S. Eliot (because he was a friend of Stravinsky) to Claudel to André Gide, even Ramuz. I tramped all over London to try to get Ramuz. But it was mainly because Stravinsky had read these books that I wanted to. I read his *Poetics of Music* and found it quite heavy going. I wrote an essay on music which must have been influenced colossally by Stravinsky's text, because the headmaster's report said, 'Not only has this boy got a phenomenal gift as a musician but he has a phenomenal intellect on the subject of music.' This, I'm afraid, all came from *Poetics of Music*, a book, by the way, I now heartily detest, clearly half written by Claudel and half by Valéry and full of formalistic fudge.

My sense of direction at this time was coming entirely from Stravinsky – including his books of conversations with Robert Craft. These I collected avidly. Everything Stravinsky did, I followed. I remember my mother taking me to Maida Vale Studios – in my mid-teens, I suppose – to hear *Perséphone*, which I fell in love with because it's such a feminine piece (there's so much of Stravinsky that's not very feminine). After this I wrote a piece in memory of Purcell, not because I liked Purcell particularly, but it sounded extremely like *Perséphone*. I later met Stravinsky at the Royal Academy of Music. Rufina Ampenoff, who was running Boosey & Hawkes at that time, gave him the score of the *Three Holy Sonnets of John Donne* (1964). Stravinsky took the score and did a curious thing: he just wrote on it, 'I know'. I don't know to this day what on earth he meant.

I got a scholarship to the Royal Academy in 1962. In a way it was a slightly depressing experience, because I'd had this marvellously inspiring teacher in Edward Chapman. I found the teachers at the Academy very clinical. They didn't teach me very much. I was still studying the piano; I studied with an ex-pupil of Arthur Schnabel who was called Guy Johnson. I didn't find him at all inspiring after Edward Chapman. But I was lucky because my grandfather knew Solomon, the pianist, who had by then had a stroke. I had lessons with him. He was totally paralysed and couldn't speak, and I remember going and playing the whole of Beethoven's Fourth Piano Concerto to him; at the end he said, 'Wonderful.' His very strict housekeeper was in the room and she said, 'Don't take any notice of that. That's the only word Mr Solomon can speak!' Anyway, I don't think anybody inspired me as much as Edward Chapman had during my years at the Academy.

The most wonderful thing that happened to me at the Academy was that my music was performed there. My opera *The Cappemakers* (1964) was a setting of one of the York Cycle of Mystery Plays in two parts that dealt with the woman taken in adultery and the raising of Lazarus. This was put on at the Academy. But previously to that the same piece had been put on at the home of Lady Birley, at Charleston Manor in Sussex. She had the most beautiful sixteenth-century tithe barn in which a music festival was held every year. She often used to have distinguished house guests. I must have been twenty and I conducted *The Cappemakers* myself. It was a semi-staged performance in the tithe barn, and because the distinguished critics Felix Aprahamian and Desmond Shawe-Taylor were there, they reviewed it: 'Composer brings beauty to mystery play'. That's all I can remember of what they said about it. I had not been taught how to conduct, I just did it.

I was taught composition by Lennox Berkeley at the Royal College of Music in London. Berkeley was a charming man, I loved him very much. I can't say that he was very important to me musically. I was not interested in studying scores or dissecting them. Neither was he. I don't think he really enjoyed teaching; he was always looking at the piece *he* was writing at the time. One always got the feeling he'd got his eye on that and was hardly concentrating on what I was doing at all. Maybe my *Piano Concerto* (1962–3) had some of the clear textures of Berkeley. His lessons were often quite amusing, because he was inordinately vague, aristocratic and very shy as well.

He used to play through Bach cantatas on occasions when I had no music to show him. He always used to encourage me. One of the most important things that came out of working with him was my exposure to his Roman Catholicism. We talked about religion and he, in his vague, shy, aristocratic way, never really got down to any kind of nitty-gritty. He just told me, 'There's a priest I know in Westminster Cathedral, Father Pemberton. I think you ought to go and see him, you know.' He also wanted me to go and study with Nadia Boulanger.

I went with my parents to Paris and went on to Fontainebleau, which is where the distinguished teacher Nadia Boulanger conducted her summer course. I went to explore the possibility of studying with her. I was very impressed by her; she was a venerable and quite remarkable old lady. But her approach, analysing Bach chorales, analysing polyphonic music, did not interest me: I was very antipathetic to the whole concept of analysis. I didn't care about those composers of the past; I just wanted to go on writing the music that I heard in my head. Analysis has never done anything for me at all. So I decided there was no point in studying with her. The person I really wanted to study with was the Australian composer David Lumsdaine.

The first, and one of the greatest, experiences of hearing my own music was when Paul Steinitz, who was the chief conductor of the London Bach Society, performed the orchestrated version of the *Donne Sonnets*. He was a very shy man, rather curt, and he said, 'I saw the first page, I knew it was a good piece, I decided to do it.' I can recall the actual sound of that piece; the spacing of the strings absolutely knocked me for six. I can still hear it in the music I write now at the age of fifty-five, some forty years later. I can still recognize the way I space chords. I recognize it much more in the *Donne Sonnets* than in subsequent pieces. It was performed in St Bartholomew the Great along with works by Britten, Nicholas Maw and Anthony Milner. Milner came up to me afterwards and said, 'Do you always write such depressing music?'

The original Donne Sonnet, which I wrote when I was fifteen, was a setting for voice and piano, or voice and organ. Later I added two more sonnets which I orchestrated. The second was 'Death be not proud, though some have called thee mighty and dreadfull'. The third one was 'I am a little world made cunningly of Elements and an Angelic spright'. It was after this performance that first I came into contact with David Lumsdaine, and I met him again at a sixtieth birthday concert for Lennox Berkeley, to which he asked all of his pupils.

David must have been some thirteen years older than me. He had come from Australia, and he had been a pupil of Matyas Seiber. At this time he was having composition lessons from Berkeley, as was Brian Ferneyhough, another modernist. Lennox used to say, 'I really don't know what to make of this music at all.' Brian was also a friend of mine and I remember going into his room one day and seeing a huge piece of forty-two-stave manuscript paper, and I said, 'Brian, why do you feel the need to fill in every stave?' And he said, 'Oh, I don't feel I've done a day's work unless I fill in every stave.'

To come back to *The Cappemakers*: I'd been given a book of the York Cycle of Mystery Plays. These plays were all created by different medieval guilds and the texts have a tremendous bite and immediacy. This attracted me very much. It had a small scoring: I remember one trumpet, one piano, one trombone, one clarinet – one of everything, almost Stravinskian scoring. The music was quite jaunty and the words have fantastic punch: 'Leap forth, let us no longer stand; she has been taken with foul adultery.' The Raising of Lazarus section in *The Cappemakers* was quite a change for me – I think there I used for the first time the sound of bells. This was really on the advice of David Lumsdaine, as was an aleatoric passage for bells, piano and for the trumpet.

My work with David had come about after Lennox's pupils had been asked to write something for his sixtieth birthday. It had to be based on what I thought was an awful piece of music, 'I do not like my looking-glass at all', from his opera *The Dinner Engagement*, a very light-hearted sort of piece. I thought the tune was absolutely appalling. Anyway, David Lumsdaine was at the concert. I was very attracted by the sounds that he made in his variation on the tune and he was obviously very impressed by my piece – I say obviously only because afterwards he came up to me and offered to teach me for nothing. It was then, I suppose, that he opened doors for me. Again, I found a teacher who had something of Edward Chapman. Even though David was a modernist he would have agreed with Schoenberg's remark: 'There's still plenty of good music to be written in C major.' I remember him saying that, and I remember him talking about the mystery of music. He opened the doors of modernism to me and he told me I would close 95 per cent of them. He was right; I did. Despite being a modernist, David was none the less able to imbue one with the sense of the mystery and magic of music – even of its sacred quality.

Benjamin Britten, who was of course a big name at this time, was not a composer I took to in the way that I took to Stravinsky. Britten was never a hero of mine, yet his vocal line attracted me and I think that is evident in *Three Sections from T. S. Eliot's Four Quartets* (1963). I think the piano part is extremely spare and possibly owes more to Stravinsky. But the vocal line was influenced by Britten.

There were no commissions at the time of the first performance of *Three Sections*. It was sung at a recital given by the eminent soprano Jennifer Vyvyan at the Wigmore Hall. I think it was at this time that the tenor Peter Pears began to take an interest in my music. He came with Lennox Berkeley to my house after they'd been to a rehearsal, and my mother put out afternoon tea on the lawn. I got to know Peter Pears quite well. Britten I met but never knew particularly well.

In those days Britten admired what I'd written and he wrote a letter to Covent Garden saying 'You ought to commission this British composer'. When Peter Pears and Britten heard *Three Sections*, Pears thought about me writing something for him, some poetry of Cavafy. This was to be prophetic of much later years – *Tribute to Cavafy* (1999).

I hate progress, I hate development and I hate evolution in most things; but in music particularly. And of course I got quite a bit of all that from David Lumsdaine. He wanted to analyse pieces like Messiaen's *Chronochromie*. But it did nothing for me; I wasn't interested in how composers worked, or how they got this or that effect. It was what I heard in the 'ear' of my musical imagination, so to speak, that guided me, that told me whether I wanted anything to do with this music. If I loved a piece the last thing I wanted to do was dissect it. I remember I was stupefied by Messiaen's *Turangalîla-symphonie* when I heard it for the first time. I was probably in the company of David Lumsdaine, who adored the piece. After that I listened and listened to it until I could no longer bear its saccharine sound world.

I have always been drawn more to the archetypal levels of human experience and human types, which is why I think I was drawn to Stravinsky and revolted by Schoenberg. Schoenberg was for me the filthy, rotten 'dirt dump' of the twentieth century. I personally could not stand the angst-ridden sound of decay in his music, the vile post-Freudian world. Basically, I do not respond to the so-called 'Germanic Tradition', whose by now rotting corpse – the hideous sound world of its fabricated complexity – smothers archetypal experience that I have always sought.

From 1961 to 1975, from the age of sixteen and through my years at the Academy, I was the organist and choir master at St John's Kensington, where I arranged performances of Bach's *St Matthew Passion*, Stravinsky's *Symphony of Psalms* and Michael Tippett's *A Child of Our Time*. I was there until my mid-thirties. Certain hymns, such as 'Lead kindly light', affected me.

I remember there was a memorial service in St Paul's Cathedral for Mahatma Gandhi which I attended. Indian classical music was being played up by the high altar, and then, without any break, at the West Door, one suddenly heard the unaccompanied cathedral choir singing 'Lead kindly light'. The combination of the two, the Indian music and Victorian English choral music, was magical.

Something of this experience later bore fruit in my *Celtic Requiem* of 1969, where in the last section the choir sing in three-part canon 'Lead kindly light'. The effect I achieved there was to do with the juxtaposition of two contrasting elements, in this case raucous children's games and the very soft sound of this English hymn.

I can't say in retrospect that the Presbyterian Church of Scotland had really meant much to me at all. But I remember the pastor and his wife, with their dark Lutheran love of Ibsen and Ingmar Bergman. I am grateful to them for imparting this love, and for allowing me to watch them die, one after the other, from cancer. I loved them deeply.

Through my connection with this church in Kensington I also met an extraordinary girl who worked a lot in South America, Mexico and Peru. One day she came to my house; I cannot think why, but she did. She gave me a Mexican cross, a Celtic cross and a Mexican poncho. I hardly knew her. She was the Roman Catholic daughter of one of the members of the congregation, yet she came out with the astonishing declaration that she had fallen in love with me and that she'd enrolled to be a nun on the same day. This girl had a tremendous effect on me. She 'opened me up', 'tore me to shreds' you might say. She in a sense started me off on a spiritual quest, which I think before this period had been only embryonically present.

She introduced me to the extraordinary mystical poetry of St John of the Cross, which of course refers so often to God as a lover. When St John of the Cross talks about his love of God, even though he may do it in the form of a love poem, there is the whole concept of transcendent love – a concept that was completely unknown to me before this time. This introduced me to something which has stayed with me ever since, the idea that there are two levels of reality – this world and the world beyond.

The pieces I wrote during this period – *Celtic Requiem* (1969), *Coplas* (1970), *Nomine Jesu* (1970) and *Ultimos Ritos* (1972) – were influenced by many things I had seen in the Roman Catholic Church. The same girl took me to the Maundy Thursday service in Westminster Cathedral. It was the first time I'd ever heard the music of Tomás Luis de Victoria, for instance, and I was immensely impressed with it. (I can still listen to it today; indeed, perhaps Victoria is the only Renaissance composer that I can stand. I love his homophony, his lack of ornament.) I remember particularly in this deeply symbolic service the moment when the altar is stripped of the sacrament which is then taken out in procession underneath a canopy. During this procession the Passiontide hymn *Pange Lingua* is sung in Latin, and then between each plainsong verse a harmonized version is sung by the boys' voices and the men's voices. The congregation followed the procession round to where the sacrament – or Christ himself – was laid to rest in the chapel of rest. This had a deep effect on me. I still think that service in the Roman Catholic Church is one of most desolate and primordially moving.

About twenty years ago I returned to it to see how it affected me and I remember it brought tears to my eyes just hearing that processional music. The utter desolation. Christ is no longer present on the altar: He had been taken away.

At this time I had begun to think that liturgy as drama and drama as liturgy were the only means of expression. I don't know whether the works I wrote at that time already expressed this, but certainly by the time that I reached *Ultimos Ritos* they had.

SHOCK TACTICS AND SOUPY TUNES

Returning to the major works of this early period, I was writing *Cain and Abel* (1965) while I was at the Academy and still studying with David Lumsdaine. It was heavily influenced by the late sacred serial pieces of Stravinsky. It was a setting from the Vulgate in Latin of the story of Cain and Abel. It is framed with Latin and then in the middle comes a melodrama which is taken from the York Cycle of Mystery Plays based on Cain and Abel. Here I used a completely different style. The setting of the Latin section is hieratical whereas the Mystery Play music is melodramatic. There's a certain wildness in it – certainly in the writing for Cain himself. At the point of Cain's killing Abel, for instance, the piece becomes aleatoric: the notes are given to the brass and they build up into a mighty fanfare.

Cain and Abel was important in so far as I think some of the lyricism of the *Donne Sonnets* appears, particularly in the last section. I remember that the critic and composer Anthony Payne wrote that *Cain and Abel* was the most impressive work he had heard since Maxwell Davies's second *Taverner Fantasia*. I knew the Maxwell Davies piece and at the time I regarded it as impressive. I don't know whether I considered Payne's comment as a compliment or not.

Next came the *Chamber Concerto* (1965), which lasts about twenty-five minutes and supports a fairly large orchestra, although I use the word 'Chamber'. It's the only abstract piece of music that I've ever written and I regard it as a total cul-de-sac, a kind of idolatry of notes for notes' sake. There is no meaning behind any of the notes. It was a purely technical exercise, rather like completing a jigsaw or filling in a crossword. I can remember it: if you asked me to go to the piano now and play it, I could, or parts of it at any rate, and little pleasure would it give me. It was much influenced by David Lumsdaine. But its abstraction, by which I mean the self-reference of its musical procedures, is something I would never return to.

The Whale (1965) started out in a rather similar way to *Cain and Abel*: again it was a hieratical setting of Latin text telling the story of Jonah and the Whale. And again there was the influence of late Stravinsky. But when I got to a certain point in *The Whale* – the storm at sea where Jonah falls into the water – I found I was composing music of a very long section that repeated different rhythmic permutations. This passage seemed almost too long in the context of a dramatic cantata. So I realized that here I was introducing a kind of surrealist element, and it needed passages to balance it, otherwise the music would be lopsided.

I had a vision in the bath one day. I leaped out of the bath; I thought: the whole piece should not begin with the telling of the story of Jonah, but it should begin with an encyclopaedic reading, a very boring encyclopaedic reading – like a newsreader, I suppose – about whales, about the sex life of whales, about the eating habits of whales, about which parts of the ocean they frequented. I rang David Lumsdaine up in the middle of the night (poor man) and, very encouragingly, he said, 'Yes, great' – he knew that this elongated storm section already existed. He said, 'Yes, yes, yes, that's a fantastic idea.' So then I went to my library and I looked for the most deliberately boring entry on whales, and found it in the *Collins Encyclopaedia*. It begins 'Marine mammal of the order Cetacea'.

There was a symbolism attached to the whale itself. The work begins with a newsreader reading this boring entry on whales, and then during this section, which lasts about four minutes, the orchestra creeps in and begins gradually to drown out the newsreader. Then it leaps into the biblical narrative in Latin of Jonah and the Whale. So we have this long four- to five-minute section at the beginning; and then we have an equivalent section after the first part of the biblical narrative when Jonah is thrown into the sea. This is when the very quiet storm happens. It lasts exactly the same length of time as the opening. So I was beginning to get the piece more balanced. After the storm it goes back to the Latin text. Then we go into the prayer that Jonah makes:

'*Clamavi de tribulatione*' ('I cried out in tribulation'). In the middle of the prayer there comes an 'avant-garde' section. But 'avant-garde' is not quite the word for it. I was in a way sticking my tongue out at what was going on in Darmstadt and in the Manchester School of Music. I mean the 'intellectual kitchens of Europe'. That ghastly, sterile, total serialization. This was an element of shock tactics. When you are in your early twenties you damned well ought to be angry and use such shock tactics.

The 'avant-garde' descent into the belly of the whale is three times the length of the other two surrealistic sections, and is a colossal outburst. (In retrospect, I think the story of Jonah and the Whale is a prefigurement of the Resurrection.) I used bells, full orchestra and organ in a kind of prefigurement of the Resurrection, because Jonah's coming out of the whale, coming out of hell, already prefigures what happened to Christ at the Resurrection. The first half of this section is the first time I had used parody in music: I parody my own material. I use the first four notes of the piece as a jazz break. I use 'harmon' jazz mutes for the trumpets; there's a kind of oompah-oompah rhythm played on trombones and bass drum; there's a wild horn section, which I remember at the time I actually pinched from a James Bond film – *Goldfinger*! So I really let anything I wanted go into this. There's a bit of plainsong, there's the sound of a fire engine, and this mighty crash of the Resurrection.

Then in the third part of this fantastical or surrealistic section the orchestra and choir are told to sing or play any note they like to indicate Jonah is coming out of the whale and landing on dry land. The music then becomes softer and softer; I take off certain instruments – the brass, the wind, the organ, the strings – and just leave the choir, until they go down to a pianissimo. This is the very end of the prayer, and the music is very lyrical, sung by a mezzo-soprano, '*Ego in voce . . .*' ('I in the voice of praise sing to God').

Then comes the final vomiting of Jonah on to the sand. This brings together the supposed surrealistic qualities of the whale and the hierarchical, ritualistic quality, because it's stamped out

– I actually ask the chorus to stamp the last final rhythmic permutations, and so it ends '*In aridam*' ('On to the dry land'). And
that was the end, plus the instruction to shout the last word,
'Ari*dam*!' In *The Whale* I was protesting, as any young man
might. But, again, it was a cul-de-sac, like all music that consid-
ers itself to be 'doing new things' – that terrible conceit and lie.

I have come back to the technique of deranging my musical
material, but for metaphysical purposes, much later in my life, at
different moments, but at this time I was trying to get myself out
of the tight formalism of late Stravinsky, although it is the late
works of Stravinsky that I care most about and which certainly
made me want to write music. The technique of deranging musical material, I thought, might help me get out of the straitjacket
of this formalism.

After completing this early group of apprentice works, I read
the French writer Jean Genet. At that time he made quite an
impression on me. I never took to his philosophy. I found it
extremely tedious. Jean-Paul Sartre wrote a huge book, *Saint
Genet*, exaggerating and often inventing the philosophy, which
was a sort of parody *via negativa* gone bonkers: pissing on the
altar and doing God knows what; it was very sacrilegious. That
did not bother me particularly, it just bored me; I didn't think it
was very interesting. What I did think was interesting in Genet
was his imagination.

I began to write an opera based on his book *Notre-Dame des
Fleurs*. My opera was mainly put together on tape, I just wrote
out a few phrases, and in a way it was the piece that came nearest to pop music. Not in the way it sounded; that was rather
unique, as I seem to remember. I used Bach chorales and I used
my own music. It was a fantastical, surreal piece of music. I've
withdrawn it, because I failed to contact Genet. Perhaps I was
unhappy to go looking for him in all the seedy bars he frequented.

My next significant work was *In Alium*, composed in 1968. It's quite a 'charming' piece – that's a fairly degrading thing to say about it. It's 'charming' because it sets the rather sentimental French Catholic poet, Charles Péguy's text 'Hope is a little girl of no importance who came into the world on Christmas day last year' (but in French).

The music is extremely sugary, extremely sentimental, certainly on the sentimental side of Roman Catholicism. It was the first piece where I used acoustic space. It was commissioned for a Promenade concert, so I decided to use the space of the Albert Hall and have four speakers placed in different positions around the Hall. There was a single, very high soprano line plus a string orchestra with Hammond organ, percussion and grand organ which I played myself.

In the last section the soprano sings a twenty-four-part canon with herself, using pre-recorded tapes. At the same time you hear children breathing gently as they fall asleep. This idea came from Péguy, but I think my use of it was surrealistic. Péguy wrote in one of his poems, 'There's nothing more beautiful in all the world than a child who falls asleep while saying its prayers.' I took this literally. I remember a wonderful old man, Eric Dougharty, Head of Stereo at the BBC, said, 'Mmmm, so you really want me to go and find a French child, a Spanish child, a Latin child, a German child, and you want them to say their prayers and go to sleep.' I went with him to find these children. Some of them were so young they actually did fall asleep. I remember a French child falling asleep saying 'Notre Père'. We had slightly more difficulty with the Latin one because children on the whole don't speak Latin any more.

The piece ends as the pre-recorded soprano parts land on a single A, so you get this wonderful pulsing sound of children sleeping and the single A from which the piece started. In the first section the tape parodies Sunday-school hymns, based on the melodic lines of the orchestra. In a similar way I parody a romantic piano solo. Then there is the middle section which has an incredibly soupy tune and I instruct the singers on tape to make sounds of clicking and sounds of kissing.

It went down very well at the Proms. The critic Edward Greenfield referred to it as the first classical musical love-in. He said he saw young couples and old couples holding hands. As to my use of acoustic space, I was very happy with it. I loved being able to hear sound coming from all round the hall. Now I don't care if I never hear it again.

In Alium was a one-off. It was written slightly tongue-in-cheek. I wanted to write it as I had a soft spot for Sunday-school hymns, but I did not want to repeat it.

The next piece that had any significance, I think, was the *Introit for March 27, the Feast of St John Damascene* (1968). In this piece I tried to get rid of all the avant-garde gimmickry and to write as pure a piece of music as I possibly could at that time. I wrote it for the London Bach Society with Paul Steinitz. I decided to base the entire piece on the long fugue at the opening of Bach's B minor Mass. Every note in the piece is informed by notes coming from this B minor Mass Kyrie, although I would not expect anybody actually to hear that. It's a very structured piece – probably the most structured that I'd written at that point. It reaches a peak in the middle with the soprano singing a high D, and then it goes back on itself. It ends with a total surprise, with the quotation of the homophonic beginning of Bach's Mass played on the strings exactly as Bach wrote it.

In this *Introit* there is, in embryo, just the beginning of the idea of my music being subsumed by something else – in this case by *somebody* else, and a far greater composer.

Introit was received by the critics with great acclaim. It was a period in my life when they were saying, 'Yes, yet another masterpiece.' If one can, I think one should be impervious to all criticism, good or bad. There is that wonderful story about a young monk in the third century, who complained that he could not stand all the criticism and praise that he was receiving. So the abba said, 'Go to the graveyard and abuse the dead, then praise them and then come back to me and tell me how they react.' So after the young monk had done this he returned to the abba, and the abba asked, 'Well, what did the dead do?' And the young monk said, 'Nothing.' The abba replied, 'Do likewise. You are also "dead".'

I worked on *Celtic Requiem* incredibly slowly. It seemed like a long period of living with the chord of E flat, rather like the beginning of *Das Rheingold*. I just lived with this chord of E flat and with the notion that I wanted to compose a piece based around it, using children's voices, very ancient Celtic poetry, and little bits of the *Missa Pro Defunctis*. I stayed in Ireland for a long time and nothing happened; I thought, nothing's ever going to happen – I always used to think that. You know the way some artists look when they go round with a gloomy face, they find it difficult to smile, difficult to do anything. I've seen it on other composers' and painters' and poets' faces. That's how I felt and looked. Then I was given a book by David Holbrook on traditional children's games.

Suddenly, I understood why the idea of children was connected with this piece: I was fascinated to learn that very ancient children's games, which are still enacted, were about death. The piece begins with a very soft sound of the chord of E flat played on the strings and then you hear children whispering, whispering, whispering, and then they gradually creep in onto the stage (it's a semi-staged piece) and they chant, rather viciously: '*Ene mena bora mee, kisca lara, mora di* – eggs, butter, cheese, bread; stick, stock, stone dead!' And whoever they point to at the word 'dead' becomes the victim who has to undergo the rite of death.

It was the children's games that got the music started and basically I regarded the children's games as the most important, the most traditional part of the piece. Looking back, this is again, very embryonically, where tradition begins to make itself apparent. By 'tradition' I mean that which is from God. Any artist concerned with the sacred must spend his life finding his way back to that *source*.

In *Celtic Requiem* there were three strands, all of them in some way traditional: there was the strand of the children's games, then there were the pointers from a few words of *Missa pro defunctis*. I set only a few of the words, just to point to where we were in the Requiem. What was most important was the children simply enacting the games on stage. Then finally there was the Celtic element which I drew from ancient Irish sources. I had a book of translations of very early Celtic poetry; the poetry of keening – 'Oh father, you have left us, where have you gone? *Ochón*' – *Ochón* being a Celtic sigh of grief.

Looking back, I see that I had not totally got rid of surrealist aspects in my music. There remained the clashing of different elements which left aspects of the music unresolved, and I most certainly had not found tradition.

I was left still looking for some kind of symbolical language. Juxtaposing Bach against my own music, or juxtaposing children's games with my own music, really did not amount to finding such a language.

When I composed *Coplas* (1970), a piece for choir and tape, I again used Bach material. *Coplas* was based on the mystical poetry of St John of the Cross and was set in Spanish. Here I use symbolism to a much greater extent; for instance, the choir had to be in a cruciform pattern. I remember how the beginning of this piece actually came to me. (I don't believe there is such a thing as chance – there is a meaning for everything that happens in life.) I was driving my car and I turned on the radio, and at that very moment came the sublime last cadence of the Crucifixus in Bach's *Mass in B Minor*. Just those closing chords. I thought, yes, I want to write a piece based on that. It took a very long time for me to write the entire piece, but those closing chords of Bach became the closing of *Coplas*. *Coplas* uses the notes of Bach's music seven times, again symbolically. A recording of the Crucifixus actually comes in and gradually subsumes my own music. This idea comes really from the mystical writings of St John of the Cross, about the annihilation of self. It was another embryonic idea that was to go much further later.

After I had written *Coplas* I was commissioned by Dartington

Hall to write and conduct a piece for their semi-amateur choir. Dartington was then under the auspices of William Glock (Controller of Music at the BBC), who was a very dear friend. I travelled all over England, and at a later date all over Greece, with William and his wife Anne. I could never take his modernism but that didn't matter; we all got on so well together.

For Dartington I wrote *Nomine Jesu* (1970) which was scored for harpsichord, chamber organ, two alto flutes, five priests (who proclaimed various texts of the Gospels relating to Christ) and chorus. Both *Coplas* and *Nomine Jesu* were to find their way into the large-scale work that I was to compose next, *Ultimos Ritos*.

The genesis of *Ultimos Ritos* (1972) was complex. Living with those two pieces, *Coplas* and *Nomine Jesu*, I found that in some way they were connected, and to begin with I couldn't figure out how. I looked at the Bach material, then at *Coplas*, and I thought, that piece suggests that it could very well have an instrumental mirror movement preceding it. So I composed an instrumental movement. I think the best music in *Ultimos Ritos* is that fourth instrumental section, the most esoteric music I had then written, '*Coplas in espejo*'.

So this instrumental section is identical in length but it moves from the end of *Coplas*, as it were, back to the beginning. It's not an exact note parallel and many people would not hear it as such, but none the less they are exact mirrors in time of each other. Then it seemed absolutely clear to me that in the middle there should be the name of Christ: '*Nomine Jesu*' ('In the name of Christ'). In this middle movement I was using a very large orchestra with many trumpets and trombones. I also had the idea of putting timpani (symbolically) at the four positions of the cathedral; one group on the right-hand side, another on the left, another at the north transept and another at the south transept. Again, as with the positioning of the choir in *Coplas*, it was in cross formation. This symbolism of the whole piece goes back to when I switched the radio on in the car: the section of the B minor Mass I heard was 'and was crucified and buried'. *Ultimos*

Ritos really is about crucifixion and burial of the self.

The first movement, written last, starts with a ferocious black chord for full orchestra and it's not just any old black chord, it's an aggregation of the notes of Bach's Crucifixus, and is particularly chromatic in its formation. I put all the notes together from bottom to top, the first note C and the second note B, the third note F, then fourth note E, then A, then F sharp, then D sharp, then G, then B flat, then C sharp, then D, then G sharp. So the movement begins with this twelve-note apocalyptic sound formed out of Bach's Crucifixus.

This violent beginning introduces the first setting of St John of the Cross with stabbing chords, on the word 'Crucifixus' sung backwards ('suxificurc'), symbolically the hammering of the nails into the Cross. This is followed by another blast of the opening chord followed by that marvellous poetry of St John of the Cross: 'One day he climbed a tree and spread his arms out so wide, his heart an open wound with love.' He wrote this when he was in prison in Spain and it comes from a secular love song. The poet does this wonderful thing of turning it into an entirely metaphysical idea, and I tried to mirror this in the music. That is why this very much quieter, much more serene passage (played on the brasses and the choir and pulsing strings, keeping very quietly that opening crucifixion chord) is rudely interrupted seven times by sopranino recorders and a little tabor drum playing a medieval Spanish folk-song. This was the first time I had used instruments to symbolize different things. I had to have a reason: why did I use trumpets? Why did I use flutes? Why did I use timpani? There had to be a reason for expressing these metaphysical concepts.

The second movement deals with the descent of the Eucharist, and I do this by having trumpets in very high galleries answering the trumpets on the floor space. I was symbolizing the heavenly and the royal (trumpets representing royalty) with the descent of the Eucharist. I also used flutes at ground level and recorders at a higher level. Traditionally flutes and recorders are the instruments of Divine Love. Gradually during this descent of the

Eucharist the sound of the chords of the original Bach on which the whole piece is based start to become audible. You leave this aggregation of notes that implied the crucifixion, and gradually the Bach begins to become audible. Then very quietly you hear the middle movement, *Nomine Jesu*. It comes in very quietly with the singing of the word 'Jesu'. The movement ends with a rhapsodic soprano solo, a setting of some of the most ecstatic words of St John of the Cross: 'I lay with my beloved amongst the lilies, there to fade.'

The idea of notes meaning something, chords meaning something, instruments meaning something, was beginning to make itself felt. I thought I really had achieved something in *Ultimos Ritos*. Critics have claimed to see the influence of Messiaen. This was something I was not aware of at the time, and on hearing it again recently I became convinced that they have been led astray by very superficial aspects.

Ultimos Ritos is certainly very dramatic, very exoteric and very 'Roman Catholic' – that whole culture of the violence of the Crucifixion. If I endeavoured to put into music the idea of the crucifixion today, I would never set it in this violent manner because I believe, with Cecil Collins, that the image of the murdered God, with the blood, the sweat and the agony of suffering, has been disastrous for the culture of the Latin West. Such a violent image may explain a great deal of the violence of Western art.

Today I regard *Ultimos Ritos* with respect. It's on the way to somewhere. But Roman Catholicism would never be able to guide me towards the harmony and balance of tradition I was seeking. I should say at this point that for some mysterious reason I *personally* could never find this in the Western tradition – neither in Western music nor in the Western Church.

This growing preoccupation with finding a way to express metaphysical concepts through musical means had really begun at the time when I first met Father Malachy, when I was twelve. He was one of the most interesting Roman Catholics I have ever met. He was in contact with Sufis and he used to invite Sufis and Methodists down to the ancient castle in Kent where he lived his last years. It was there that I first met Metropolitan Anthony from the Orthodox Church.

Father Malachy was an extraordinary man, very Irish, with all the vagueness of the Irish. But the whole idea of tradition was very important to him. All round the castle he had little notices encouraging us to keep alive the medieval spirit in art, and he spoke to me a lot about that kind of thing, so it was not surprising that the *Little Requiem for Father Malachy Lynch* (1972) came to me fully born; the first time this happened to me. At his funeral, an open-air funeral in Aylesford Priory, the idea of the first section of the Requiem had already come to me. As I walked away and drove home to London the music began to unfold in my head. This has happened to me on a number of occasions since, where music appears to be given as a parting gift from the dead person.

After Father Malachy's death, I felt that I wanted to write an opera based on St Thérèse of Lisieux; this intense twenty-four-year-old saint who appears to do nothing at all during her earthly existence.

Around this time I was introduced to the Irish playwright Gerard McLarnon. I got on very well with him. He was Orthodox, and he vehemently hated Roman Catholicism from his childhood in Ireland. All his plays reflected this loathing – many of them are blasphemous, many of them very funny. However, he was a very deep man: he read Homer every day of his life; Dostoevsky was his favourite author; he loved the Greeks, he loved the Russians. He was a wonderful, remarkable man – I miss him very much. He had a violent temper and we came to physical blows over this opera. But most importantly he deepened my interest in the Orthodox Church.

When Gerry first took me into an Orthodox church I just felt as if I was at home. I also remember going to an art exhibition with him and I was drawn to just one painting. It looked like a painting to me, but it was an ikon, and I was totally awed by it. I remember thinking at the time that in this ikon, time and nature are somehow *made new*.

I should say that Father Malachy had already influenced me in this direction: he said to me, 'It's the Eastern Church that you should go towards.' He also said, which is very unusual for a Roman Catholic, 'You know, John, the Roman Catholic Church is a fading star.' Was he hinting that in every aspect of life and art dogma could no longer serve as a guide? Maybe he thought the sort of legalism, the scholasticism of Roman Catholicism was not for me. He was right. As a Romanian Orthodox monk said to me recently, 'After Christ, there is no Law, we have only our conscience left.'

When I mentioned the subject of Thérèse to Gerry, he said, 'Oh God – which one? Not that awful Little Flower. It must be Teresa of Avila.' And I said, 'I'm afraid it's not – it is what you call that awful Little Flower.' In the end he could see why I wanted to do it, because of her huge crisis of faith at the age of twenty-three, or twenty-four, when she was dying. She reached a stage of near nihilism and it was then, or soon after, that she made the extraordinary statement that she would spend her eternity doing good on earth. I remember asking Father Malachy what Thérèse of Lisieux did, and he said, 'She didn't do anything. But what she does now is a different matter.'

Progress on the libretto of *Thérèse* (1973–6) was slow and painful. Gerry had never worked with a composer before; I had never worked with a librettist. Also a certain difference in temperament hindered us, although we were very close at one level. He wanted to bring in the literary figure of Arthur Rimbaud, because he could see a parallel. This was partly because Rimbaud wrote all his greatest poetry at the same age that Thérèse was undergoing her spiritual crisis. He wanted this rather wild character to act as a kind of psychopomp.

These differences of temperament between Gerry and me, and the fact that I didn't react very much to worldly drama, made for considerable difficulty. Gerry's plays, though intensely and fiercely dramatic, had nothing to do with liturgy or liturgical drama, which was what interested me. What he suggested would have led to a libretto that would have been a distillation of a Dostoevsky novel, which just did not suit me.

We seemed to be getting nowhere at all so I called in Clive Wearing, scholar and conductor of Lassus, who acted as a kind of catalyst. Clive knew nothing about the Eastern Church but about the Roman Church and Roman liturgy he knew a great deal. He understood our problem intellectually and I always needed the support of an intellectual figure in these early years.

Clive immediately saw the possibility of using the Song of Songs, because of Thérèse's deeply erotic connection to Christ. She was, after all, only twenty-four and she saw Him as a bridegroom. As soon as Clive mentioned the Song of Songs I immediately started writing. I began with the end, rather as I did with *Ultimos Ritos*. I began with their love duet, with Christ singing – again I wanted to use space – Christ singing from the heavens, Thérèse singing on stage, and their music coming closer and closer together until they became unified. Having written that, I could then begin to write the first part, where she coughs up blood; she sees that she's going to die and believes there is nothing but a void, a state of total annihilation. This first section owes a great deal to Gerry's passion for Greek tragedy. Incidentally, one of the nuns of the Carmelite Convent in Lisieux, who remembered Thérèse's sister, told me it was total atheism that she experienced in those last days of her life.

Having composed the metaphysical love duet I was then able to fragment it, so that at the beginning of the opera there appears its complete opposite, Thérèse's divine darkness, where she was plagued by demons calling her an atheist, hissing and terrifying her. Two large sections of the piece, the end and the beginning, were now written. Then I found it much easier to introduce some kind of dramatic relief between these intensely static and hieratical sections. Rimbaud comes on, blasphemous, drunk, and everything about him is uncontrolled and dangerous, and he in fact leads Thérèse on spiritual journeys with her father, who symbolizes Christ. The father/Christ leads her through various journeys where in one of them she prays for a murderer, very Dostoevskyan, because at the last minute the murderer kisses the Cross and she sees that as a sign from heaven, like the repentant thief on the Cross at Christ's crucifixion. Then, in her afterlife, we see her on the battlefields of the First World War, and finally witnessing the end of the world. She prostrates on the dust and the mystical love duet then begins, emerging out of the total abyss.

I think I wrote myself out of what I saw as the spiritual 'angst' of Roman Catholicism by the act of composing *Thérèse*. I detested the Roman Church's legalism and scholasticism, and I felt Christianity had to be so much more than I had as yet discovered. The worldliness of the Roman Church, and the pharisaical Vatican, papal infallibility, seemed to me the acme of human pride – the terrible heresy that had tortured, and was to continue to torture mankind for a long time to come.

At the same time I wanted to remove from my mind the angry, tortured face of Schoenberg with his rotting humanism and his humanly contrived techniques – which none the less I had used in *Thérèse*. I wanted to rid myself of such mechanisms once and for all.

True, in the *Introit* and *Ultimos Ritos* I had in a sense allowed my own voice to be annihilated by Bach's music. Bach, after all, was human. He had something to do with the Divine but he was certainly not the Divine Voice. Mine was still a Western, formulaic way of writing sacred music. This was not a real annihilation of the self because it came from outside; it was *exoteric*. I had to go much much deeper into myself. I had to gradually annihilate the personal emotions and the conscious deliberation in my music. I had gone as far as I could possibly go in that direction in *Ultimos Ritos*; I had to pause now and try to stop thinking for a while. I needed to 'lay aside all worldly care'.

As St Gregory of Nazianzen has said, 'I shared in the image of God, but did not keep it safe.' I had hardly begun to write *true music*. And as St John Chrysostom has said, 'When you are uncertain, when you have nowhere to lean or to stand firm, then indeed you are more certain because it is only God who is a support and strength.' I only realize this now with hindsight. I also realize that I had become 'absolutist' in my rejection of Western Christianity and Western music. But again with hindsight, I also see that to believe that there is no richness in a Haydn quartet (for example) and that not a word of Aquinas or Calvin ever once rang true is clearly myopic and ignorant. None the less, at this period in my life, I *had* to be 'absolutist'. Maybe later I could become more embracing.

FROM ROME TO PATMOS

Thérèse was premièred at Covent Garden on 1 October 1979. None the less this was a very difficult period in my life because I had been so totally disillusioned by Western civilization and Western culture. I hadn't any concrete path to follow. Also, I had not so far met Indian musicians; I had not come across Byzantine chant, I had not heard the music of the Sufis. So I was in a void; which wasn't a bad thing.

My collaboration with Gerard McLarnon went on, and he produced quite soon after *Thérèse* a libretto that I immediately reacted to, having in the meantime got used to his rather violent dramatic sense. It was based on Dostoevsky and I feel I owe a debt to Dostoevsky; he and the great Greek writer Papadiamandis are the only two novelists I can read. Gerry produced a libretto based on Dostoevsky's short story *A Gentle Spirit*, which is about a pawnbroker who sees a forlorn young girl selling all her trinkets and finally an ikon, and he is appalled by the fact that she would actually trade in the Holy Mother of God. Finally she jumps out of the window holding the ikon.

A Gentle Spirit (1977) worked very well and even went on a long tour. It was more angst-ridden than anything I'd written until then, far more so than *Ultimos Ritos*. But it was a different kind of angst, it wasn't a Schoenbergian, German angst, it was more Russian. It had an Orthodox dimension. The sort of angst I hear in Tchaikovsky, all of whose work I love.

I can see, of course, with hindsight, the great temptation and attraction of Mahler's angst-ridden style. The self-inflated yearning of the ego, the fragmentation, the post-Freudian psychology and the confusion in his music that burns man up in body and spirit, mirror something of the emotional and spiritual alienation of our times. The peak of humanism in music had occurred some two hundred years before in Handel, with an almost Sophoclean sense of tragedy, dignity, objectivity, transparency and his astounding simplicity that, as it were, lays bare our pretensions. No wonder Schoenberg dismissed him. From Beethoven (who called Handel 'the greatest composer of all – I kneel at his tomb') to Wagner (who said 'Handel draws blood'), and on to Mahler and Schoenberg and Berg, humanism was going rapidly downhill.

The corpse, as it were, of this humanism was still present in my own music when I wrote another anguished piece but one more connected to the whole concept of sacrifice, the walling-up of Antigone, which was a dark subject but had a deep metaphysical undertone. I composed rather slowly and laboriously during this period, and though I still quite like *A Gentle Spirit* and *The Immurement of Antigone* (1978) I could now live very well without them. Both these and *Thérèse* were based on a system that was incapable of satisfying me.

I became Orthodox in 1977. A number of things brought this about. First of all, as I have said, I was deeply disillusioned by the Roman Catholic Church, by its legalism and also (as Father Malachy seemed to have hinted) by the way in which it seemed to be going downhill in its drift towards humanism. Even at its best, the ultramontane variety of Catholicism did not appeal to me because of the scholasticism. I thought, there simply must be *more*. I'd had instructions from a priest at Westminster Cathedral, but I profoundly distrusted the proselytizing attitude. I recall the priest saying, 'I think it's time for you to come in, I think you should come, Our Lord wants you.' The Orthodox are quite the opposite: they try to push you away. So that attracted me towards the Orthodox Church.

Through knowing Gerry, I got to know Metropolitan Anthony of Zourozh who was at that time the Exarch, head of the Russian Orthodox Church in the West, and I began to go to talks with him. He is a considerable spiritual force and a complex man. He had been a doctor; he took secret monastic vows when he was working with the Resistance in France during the Second World War; he had been an atheist, until his mother made him go and listen to a Russian Orthodox priest. He came back and his mother said, 'Well, what did you make of that?' and he said, 'I want nothing more to do with religion. I want nothing to do with it.' His mother persuaded him to read one of the Gospels, and he said, 'All right, what's the shortest?' And I think she said St Mark, and after reading the first page of St Mark he was aware of the presence of Christ at the end of the table. And this experience really changed this man for the rest of his life.

I remember on my first visit saying, 'Well, my life's like this, like this and like that – pretty ghastly, isn't it?' And he said, 'Yes.' And from then onwards we met almost weekly. I was lucky enough to get the very best of him when he was strong, in his sixties, and very fit. But the big difference in the conversations with him and his Roman Catholic counterparts was that there was no formal catechism. In fact he never mentioned the word 'God' in all my conversations with him. He really told me a series of anecdotes. I recall one in particular that has come back in my life in various ways to help me.

His mother, he told me, worried a lot, and so one day he decided to give her a mantra-like saying. He said to her, 'Well, you just keep saying, all day long, "I don't care about anything at all, I don't care about anything at all."' And she did this, and then a couple of days later he came into his mother's room and she was still saying, 'I don't care about anything at all.' She turned to him and said, 'What is it I don't care about?' I still feel tremendously privileged to have heard all these anecdotes.

When I'd been going to talks with him for maybe a year and a half, he suddenly said 'Now I think it's time for you to come into the Church and I want to talk to you about something serious.' I thought at this point he was going to talk about God, but he didn't. He said, 'I want you to make a setting of the Orthodox Liturgy of St John Chrysostom, but I want you to know nothing about the sacred tone systems of the Orthodox Church. I want you to have a totally spontaneous reaction to the text.' He did me a great favour by doing this, because I didn't know a single thing about the sacred tone systems, and I set it as simply as I possibly could so that the words would not be obscured.

Of course, musically it was my own fabrication and when it was sung liturgically it threw the cat among the pigeons. People came up to me and said, 'What's that supposed to be? It's just your own fabrication, it's your own music. It's got nothing to do with tradition.' 'How could you set that like that? It's not in the right tone.' I didn't know what they were talking about – 'not the right tone: that should have been in Tone 4, that should have been in Tone 2, that should have been in Tone 6 – it's just your fabrication.' It was the first time I'd really heard the word 'tradition' and it really pierced me.

As to why Metropolitan Anthony wanted me deliberately to be ignorant of the tones, I can only hazard a guess. Maybe he thought it was a very good way for me to learn the liturgy, or maybe he anticipated this would happen. He is a complicated man; he always does things in a rather round-about way. It could well have been a way to bring me face to face with tradition. But I must say that at this stage of my life I felt I did not want to write any more music for a very long time. Indeed it questioned what I had been doing all these years. All this music, all this modernist influence – even Mozart, even Beethoven, even Bach – they did not have tradition in the sense that the Eastern Church had tradition. I was certainly silent for a while. What little I did write I found painful to do.

Somehow I had to understand the true meaning of tradition for myself. Nothing else would do. All non-traditional music seemed to me contrived, concerned with satisfying the ego, and to have nothing, absolutely nothing to do with the sacred. Grasping the implications of this took me some considerable time. I certainly did not understand it to begin with. I don't now.

I thought – with hindsight, wrongly – that I had to do something about this crisis, rather than just letting a long period of time elapse before really comprehending what tradition is. I certainly did not think I could get it from books. It was something that just took years to comprehend, to meditate on, in order to understand. Most people know little or nothing about tradition in the musical world so I could look for no help in that direction. Probably I thought one of the most wonderful things about tradition at this point was the fact that it was non-progressive, there was no development and there was no evolution: it was something that was eternal, it meant that such a thing as innovation simply was not valid. Innovative music by a human being was nothing; it did not exist at all in the spiritual realm.

Looking back, I think I understood what Father Anthony was saying from a Christian point of view. When you write something, if you believe you are created in the image of God, then music in a sense comes from God. It's very well put by St Paul, when he says, 'It is no longer I who live but Christ who lives in me.' And you could reinterpret that: 'It is no longer I who live, but tradition that lives in me', because tradition is God, at its highest point. Therefore, in practice, it should be no longer 'I' who 'composes' but tradition that composes in me. But at this point, how any understanding of tradition related to my music I had yet to fathom out.

It must be understood that Metropolitan Anthony couldn't have cared less about any crisis I might have been experiencing as a composer. He was very anti-art – certainly with me. Being a complicated man, I think if he was talking to somebody who hated art, he would probably have said he loved it. But he did not want me to be seduced by ikons or music. I didn't entirely agree with him about that. I even remember saying to him, 'Sometimes you say you don't want the ikons in the church, you don't want the music because the music gets in the way, you'd like to have total silence. You are a Quaker.' 'No, no,' he retorted.

It was Metropolitan Anthony who received me into the Orthodox Church in 1977.

With the whole business of being converted to the Russian Orthodox Church on the one hand, and tradition being very much in the front of my mind on the other hand, I thought I'd explore the Russian aspect first of all. I read a book on Gogol, a lot of Dostoevsky and a huge biography of Tolstoy. What impressed me about Gogol was that towards the end of his life he suddenly discovered tradition, and people say he went mad. I can understand that. When you have been writing your own music for, let's say, twenty-eight years or so, and suddenly members of a congregation come up and tell you you're not writing in tradition, it stops you in your tracks. I began to question the whole Western concept of art altogether. And, going back to Gogol, he reached this crisis at the *end* of his life by discovering tradition. He took all his novels and tried to insert the sacred into them, insert tradition into them. Can you imagine, if I'd gone on writing pieces like *The Whale, Ultimos Ritos,* etc., etc., and then suddenly decided I'd got to insert Orthodox tradition into these pieces?

So I concerned myself with all things Russian. For instance, I made some settings of Russian folk-songs. Despite my current love of all things Greek, I entered by the Russian door of Orthodoxy because to begin with its chant is more familiar to the Westerner. Also, I entered the Russian Orthodox Church in England because at that time it had this charismatic figurehead: that was the Church to which the converts went. The Greek Church in 1977 was isolated; it was very much its own church and there were hardly any English converts. Also, in the Russian Church they sang half the service in English and half the service in Church Slavonic. Metropolitan Anthony always used to preach in English. That was the reason I entered through the Russian Church.

I remember vividly that first year I became Orthodox. I remember the musical impressions. People have said that I came in through music, but that is not totally true because I don't particularly love the Bortniansky, Rachmaninov kind of Russian church music. I love things like Znamenny chant; a chant of the Middle Ages. The very first time I went to all the services in Holy Week – Monday, Tuesday, Wednesday, Thursday, Friday, Saturday – there was a lot of this unaccompanied Znamenny chant. Tears came into my eyes that had nothing to do with human emotion. I don't know what you'd call them, but they had nothing to do with joy and they had nothing to do with sorrow. In a sort of way they were tears of joy/sorrow, a mixture of the two. There was a deep, timeless compunction in this chant.

The first composition that reflected my awareness of tradition and Orthodoxy was a piece that had a title that came from the Fathers. It was a Greek title, *Kyklike Kinesis* (1977), and it was about the journey of the soul, the introduction to the spiritual life, the practical application of it and then 'theosis' ('deification'). It was a huge subject. I didn't really succeed with the piece. The London Sinfonietta commissioned it. For an orchestra that was concerned exclusively with modernism to be confronted with a piece entitled *Kyklike Kinesis* ('circular movement') at that time must have been a bit of a shock. But my musical idiom hadn't really changed – serialism and systems were still knocking about. I don't dislike the piece now. I just think I got absolutely nowhere near comprehending in music what I had read of the Fathers.

At this time I also wrote another piece, *Palintropos* (1978), which is again rather on the fringe of Orthodoxy. I went to Patmos and I remember sitting outside the monastery in Patmos all day long and watching the different colours on the sea and having a long conversation with a monk. Out of that came a piece which is related to the landscape. It is related to Orthodoxy by way of the Orthodox belief – unlike the Roman Catholics – that Man and Nature are basically divine on account of the Incarnation. The Catholic and Western Church in general see man and nature as basically sinful. The fact that *Palintropos* was influenced by Nature, the nature of Patmos, I think was in a sense Orthodox. But I was still nowhere near tradition. I was still lost and still searching. *Palintropos* is the only piece of mine that ever came near to being a Debussyan tone poem.

Of the *Akhmatova Requiem* of 1979, I certainly thought when I wrote it, 'this is the best of me' (as Elgar said about *The Dream of Gerontius*). I do not think that now, but I still think it's a key piece. Again it's not traditional but it has connections with Orthodoxy, particularly with Russian Orthodoxy, because it sets the Requiem which Akhmatova wrote in memory of all those mothers who lost their sons, and all those who were persecuted in the Stalin purges.

In the *Requiem* I did use the tones; in *straight* quotes from the funeral service, another quote straight from the Orthodox Resurrection Service on Easter Night and another from the Orthodox Good Friday Service. But they are absolutely straight quotes. The rest of the music is still composed in a contrived idiom. But what I love so much about it is how it shows that what I had acquired from modernism since David Lumsdaine had introduced me to it was beginning to vanish. It's far closer in the darkness of its harmonic spacing and in the scoring of brass, timpani, bells, tam-tams and strings to the *Donne Sonnets* of 1962. I did not want to make a political statement in this piece. The *Requiem* is really a meditation on death. I certainly thought at the time, this is very truly in my voice, in the same way I had thought about the *Donne Sonnets*; I felt much less easy about things being in my own voice when the demon, modernism, was lurking around. But even so I had not found 'The Voice' yet.

The *Akhmatova Requiem* is extremely monumental in character. It lasts about an hour, with soprano solo singing almost uninterruptedly throughout, with the exception of the bass solo intonings of Orthodox prayers for the dead. I wrote it in Russian and I worked with Father Sergei Hackel, who was professor of Russian and Slavonic Studies at Sussex University and a deeply intelligent person. We used to meet in a friend's penthouse near Victoria Station once a week and he would go through it line by line so that I got the true feeling of the Russian text. I was very drawn to Akhmatova's poetry at this time because it was extremely simple, and there were very stark statements of fact – it had no frills. In that sense it was deeply Russian. Nothing I'd ever written except the *Chamber Concerto* was totally secular. You could say that I treated it, whenever I could, and as far as the text allowed, in a sacred manner, because I'm incapable of doing anything else. I inserted the prayers; they're not in the original Akhmatova poems.

Gennadi Rozhdestvensky conducted it superbly at the première. He wanted to see what it was like first; I gave him one of my first sketches – I hadn't put any bars in it, I hadn't got any rests in it – and he said, 'This is the only score I want; I'm going to work with this.' When, later, my publishers Chester's presented a published score to him, with bar lines and all the rest of it, he said, 'I don't want this, I don't want this one. I'll work from your original.' And then he said, 'Look, I have a picture of Akhmatova, of Stalin, and an ikon of Christ. This means so much to me.' He chose to perform it for his last concert as chief conductor of the BBC Symphony Orchestra, first at Edinburgh on 20 August 1981 and then seven days later at his farewell concert at the Proms in London.

In the event the tomblike structure of the piece was just too much for the audience and there was a mass walk-out. I was sitting there beside Sergei feeling extremely uncomfortable as many of the audience walked past me. Of course Akhmatova's poetry was not allowed to be published in Russia at that time. Rozhdestvensky was taking one hell of a risk in doing it at all. In fact when he went back to Russia he was stopped at Customs and asked to produce the score. Curiously, although it was unpopular with the audience, it was very popular with the critics.

Because of my continuing questioning of the whole basis of Western art, all I really wanted to do was to disappear to a Greek island and just think and write *if* music came to me.

*

The most radical piece that I wrote after the *Akhmatova Requiem* was to be *Prayer for the World* (1981). It is based on the Orthodox Hesychast tradition, the prayer of silence, known as the Jesus Prayer: 'Lord Jesus Christ, Son of God, have mercy upon me, a sinner.' Paradoxically, it was commissioned by Contemporary Music Network, and I knew it was going to be performed alongside a work by Arnold Schoenberg. In writing *Prayer* I'd still not properly embraced tradition, or found 'The Voice', but in it I went as far as I could go at that time.

Prayer lasts nearly an hour, it's extremely hairshirted, extremely quiet, but it has a sort of changing dissonance about it, the only text being the Jesus Prayer, sung in Slavonic, English and Greek. These revolve, round and round and round, still using a matrix of ever-changing notes. Mine was a totally non-developmental kind of serialism altogether, treating the Jesus Prayer as a mandala. The great ascetics and the saints are able to pray this prayer all through the day, whatever they are doing, even if they're gardening or whilst sleeping at night. The prayer never stops, and so it becomes part of their breathing – 'Lord Jesus Christ, Son of God, have mercy upon me, a sinner.' I told the choir to breathe in on the words 'Lord Jesus Christ, Son of God' and to exhale on 'have mercy upon me, a sinner'.

When I showed it to the conductor, John Alldis, he said, 'Well, there's nothing for the choir to do. My choir's very extrovert – they like to sing loudly, they like to shout occasionally, let rip. Nothing happens in *Prayer for the World* – it just rotates.' It wasn't easy to sing either, and I remember wanting to disappear through the floorboards after the performance. But I had to go on to a party to confront a posse of modernist pundits, desperate to uncork their first bottle of sparkling white wine. All I wanted to do was to get out of the hall as quickly as possible, because nobody was saying anything to me at all. Nobody said how 'nice' the piece was. I didn't expect that they would, because it wasn't 'nice'.

I wish it could be given a performance in its right setting, in its *temenos* – a Greek Orthodox church or a Russian Orthodox church, or simply with candles in a barn with a resonant acoustic. I wish somebody would take it up, even though its hairshirtedness would make it difficult for an average cathedral choir in this country. There's nothing soft about it. It is severely ascetic and was a watershed in my life.

I would say this was the first piece of mine that had nothing to do with entertaining an audience, nothing do to with the concert hall: it was a prayer. I was beginning to organize my music according to a different order of ideas and maybe a higher order of reality. It was from this piece onwards that I found myself abandoning Western musical procedures and the whole idea of development and I realized it was something that simply did not interest me – the whole idea of progress or evolution.

For a time after *Prayer for the World* I didn't really have or want an audience. This was a period when I simply felt I had to go right out on a limb. I was reading the *Philokalia*, the *Apophthegmata* and many other traditional books, both Islamic and Hindu. I really wanted to write liturgical music. You cannot call *Prayer for the World* exactly liturgical, although I think it could take place in any church and act as a support for meditation. There was no precedent for *Prayer*, in the sense that no one had ever attempted to realize the prayer of silence in sound before. I thought it would simply be dismissed by the critics and not comprehended at all. But Peter Stadlen, who was an intelligent man (the kind of critic we rarely see nowadays), gave it a very good review, even if he didn't understand what I was trying to do, or where I was coming from. He was impressed by the sound of it, describing it as a kind of 'silent music'.

UNCREATED EROS: UNCREATED LIGHT

In the *Great Canon of St Andrew of Crete* of 1981, I began to get pretty near to writing a piece of Orthodox liturgical music. The *Great Canon* lasts about fifteen minutes; it contains long passages of chant, some of which comes from the Middle Ages – Znamenny. It's a long musical prostration. The text is extremely penitential: 'Have mercy upon me, Oh God, have mercy upon me.' I set this for eight-part choir coming, chromatically and massively, down and down: in between are the deeply, deeply penitential writings of St Andrew. The *Canon* begins, 'Where shall I make my beginning to mourn the deeds of my wretched life?', continuing, 'Instead of Eve of the body, I have Eve of the mind. Instead of Cain of the body, I am full of murderous thoughts' – this kind of deep penitence with which the Orthodox Church begins Lent.

I was nervous about the première, because it was to be performed in Winchester Cathedral, and this kind of untamed penitential text is not exactly Anglican. In the event the piece did seem to make quite an impression on people.

Whether the Orthodox Church will ever use it in their liturgy remains to be seen. I think they ought to but I've no idea if they ever would. I would love to have been a kind of small-town Bach working for the English Orthodox Church. Maybe an autocephalous English Orthodox Church will exist one day. It is my greatest dream.

While on the subject of liturgical music, several years later I came to set the *Orthodox Vigil Service* (1984), the largest and longest piece of liturgical music I've ever written. The Vigil Service precedes the Liturgy and it contains both vespers and matins. I've always thought it to be one of the most profound services in the Orthodox Church. In monasteries the vespers would have been sung when the sun was going down, and matins might well have started early in the morning, in the middle of the night, going on to the Liturgy itself. I had to know a lot about Orthodox liturgical practice in order to come anywhere near to setting it. Father Michael Fortounatto (probably the greatest living expert on Russian chant) was an enormous help to me. He had libraries full of Russian chant, and he talked to me a lot about the meaning of the Vigil Service; where there was a peak, where it remained on one level. He also talked a lot about the Russian tones.

I began to think I couldn't even start writing in an Orthodox tone system. I reckoned that if I had a hundred or two hundred years to live it might have been a possibility. But for an Orthodox tone system to emerge in any one country takes hundreds of years. So it was a very difficult thing to do, because I had to cope with the tones which are the sacred basis of every single Orthodox service. I was not going to have another fiasco like I'd had with *The Liturgy of St John Chrysostom*. This time I wanted to go deeply into the metaphysics of the Vigil Service as well as the structure and the way it was put together. I also wanted to know about the tones. Father Michael said, 'Well, I think the best thing for you to do is to limit yourself to certain tones, because you won't be able to do it otherwise.' By then I was beginning to understand how the tones worked, after these long discussions with Father Michael.

I went away trying to take in everything he had said, and the result seemed to come out as something digested, something new. Not because of anything I had done; it became new because the tones had become part of me by some mysterious alchemical process. It didn't sound Russian, it didn't sound Greek; it had an English quality about it. The whole service, which took two and a half hours, was celebrated by Bishop Kalistos in Christ Church Cathedral, Oxford, in May 1985. As it was an Anglican church, we had erected a series of ikons for the occasion, with candles. Bishop Kalistos came up to me afterwards and said, 'This is the music we *ought* to be singing in the Orthodox Church in England, but you're a lone voice, and I'm afraid this will not happen for years because the Orthodox Church moves at a snail's pace.'

It was celebrated also in Norwich Cathedral a year later, and it was celebrated again by an Orthodox priest-monk. Perhaps one of the most dramatic occasions was in Washington Cathedral in 1988 when the Russian Church was celebrating one thousand years of being Orthodox. They celebrated it fully, with

Orthodox priests and bishops, in the presence of Metropolitans from all over Russia and Greece. It was an extraordinary and wonderful occasion. I just wish there was a real future for my Orthodox Vigil Service because I felt I had really begun to comprehend something of the deep meaning of the Orthodox tradition. Here was an English Orthodox service, although parts of it were in Greek and parts were in Church Slavonic. But looking towards any possible future, I think that an English Orthodox Church should keep to the marvellous tradition of boys and men in the choir. The Greeks have their musical language, the Russians evolved their own, and the English would have to do the same, borrowing perhaps from Russian, Arabic, Coptic, Greek or Celtic sacred traditions.

During this period of total isolation from the contemporary music circuit, and indeed the musical public, I met someone who was to become a very close and beloved friend. It all started, I recall, with a phone call from the painter and visionary Cecil Collins after he had been to a performance of *Thérèse*. He rang me up one day and said he'd like to meet me. I met him in his tiny flat in Paultons Square with his wife Elisabeth and immediately we were united by a deep empathy. He adored music; he told wonderful stories – exaggerating slightly – about listening to Stravinsky play his Piano Concerto in the Queen's Hall, with only his wife, himself and one critic there. I think Stravinsky was not very popular at that time!

I found Cecil a fount of wisdom and just the person I needed to meet at this time, because of the direction in which my music was going. He was a semi-traditionalist. His paintings were not totally traditional but there was a very strong traditional element in them, and he certainly knew a good deal about tradition. He introduced me to the great Sufi poet, Rumi; we had conversations about recent works of Stockhausen – he even communicated by letter with Stockhausen. We talked about Arvo Pärt, because around that time Pärt's music was being heard for the first time in this country and being dismissed by the establishment basically as a big yawn. I knew they were wrong and so did Cecil. I also met Marco Pallis, the Buddhist spiritual travel-writer and traditionalist. Cecil also introduced me to the great traditionalist writers; René Guénon, Ananda Coomaraswamy and Frithjof Schuon. Their writings astonished me, and gave me courage to go on.

During this period, however, it was taking me a long time to find anybody that I could collaborate with because I wanted to write about the fourth-century prostitute saint, St Mary of Egypt. It was a very difficult subject to tackle because the first part of her life was given to prostitution, although she never took money. It was basically an enormous appetite – a kind of appetite for love, one might say. It was as if she knew no other way to give love. And then she went on a pilgrimage – not because she wanted to go on a pilgrimage but because she could make love to more sailors on the boat.

I sometimes despaired of ever finding the right person who could collaborate with me on the subject of Mary of Egypt, but in the meantime I enjoyed my almost daily contact with Cecil.

Since John of the Cross, Rumi impressed me more than anybody else. I was to discover later connections between Rumi and St Simeon the New Theologian. But listening to Sufi music with Cecil I discovered a quality of innocence beyond the Fall; music so beautiful and with such a simplicity when played on the *nāy*, the Persian flute. Cecil also took me to see the Whirling Dervishes; and Kathleen Raine, the poet and scholar, who owned the house that Cecil lived in, introduced me to the Dagar Brothers, who played and sang one of the most sacred forms of Indian music, the *dhrupad*. Kathleen Raine also introduced me to Samavedic chant, the sung *veda* of the *Rig Veda*, which is even more ancient and even more sacred. Suddenly, everywhere I looked I was surrounded by people who understood tradition. I'd left the world of Western music altogether during this period. This music was like Ithaka; she had given me a marvellous journey and without her I would not have set out, but now, it seemed, she had nothing left to give me.

Petros Morosinis was also an important friend at this time. I was introduced to him by Cecil and Elisabeth Collins; or rather introduced to his wife initially because he was a recluse. He had a tremendous influence on me, even though he was not a musician by profession; he was a poet and an incredibly learned man. He'd led a rather wild youth but now lived in great simplicity on the Greek island of Aigina, reading the Fathers and becoming an expert on tradition. The fact that he was so interested in music as well was wonderful.

I played him pieces like *Ultimos Ritos* and he said, 'That is marvellous, but it is still Western and scholastic.' He also said that Stravinsky's *Canticum sacrum* was as far as a Western man could possibly go spiritually. But of course, he went on, 'there's much, much further to go and one cannot compare those Western composers, even Bach, with the music of the East'. At this time he was quite fanatical – he's much less fanatical now and even listens to Schumann! At the time we met he thought music should have no harmony and that there should be no counterpoint. Once he said to me, 'What are you writing? Sing it to me.' And I said, 'Well, I can't, Petros, I can't sing it to you – I haven't got a piano.' He said, 'Any music that's worth anything at all should be able to be sung.' He had a sort of petulant, pugilistic manner. But, damn it, I did sing it to him in the end; I managed to get the music across. And I remember later thinking that he was *right*: if music can't be sung, then it ceases to be music. It certainly ceases to be sacred music. Sacred music must be able to be in some way sung, because from a Christian point of view the Word must be heard. Music is the extension of the Word, not a frilly decoration of the Word. It is at the service of the Word, as in all great traditions. There must be no harmony, no counterpoint, just a single melodic line with an *ison*, or the tonic note of the melody, representing eternity, at least according to Petros; and, I might add, according to the entire Greek Orthodox Church.

However, to be able to do this now, *totally*, after all that has happened in music, I think is only possible in the hands of a saint. In a certain sense music has 'fallen' after the Fall of Man. But there must be the possibility that music, because of the Incarnation, can also become 'deified' here and now. That does not necessarily mean a return to chant, but it does mean something very like that, something transparent, something timeless, like chant.

My friendship with Petros gave me something unique. With his love of music I always left Aigina inspired, despite his extremely dogmatic view that music without an *ison*, or music with harmony or counterpoint, was just domestic contrivance. Moreover, the only music of any real sacred quality was music, for instance on the unaccompanied *nāy*, or the music of Byzantium, or indeed the music of all the great traditions of the East. He was not prepared to accept Western music at all, at that time. And I went away stimulated, encouraged, and fired to try to approach this apparently impossible task.

The Lamb (1982) came to me spontaneously and complete. I read Blake's poem 'The Lamb' from the *Songs of Innocence*, and as soon as I read it, the music was there. Within a quarter of an hour, the piece was finished. This was not the first time a piece had come to me in that way, without any premeditation. There were many subsequent times. Also, symbolism in the use of chords appears in *The Lamb* – there's a joy/sorrow chord in it, on the word 'Lamb', which I was to use many times later.

I had an instinct that the piece would be a great popular success. I played it to my father, and he said, 'That's very beautiful. You ought to get Chester's to send it to King's.' It was a day in late October and I rang up Chester's and they said, 'Oh, they'll have the Carol Service completely planned by now, no way will they do it.' And I said, 'No, no, no, send it, send it, send it.' Anyway, they sent it and, by Jove, immediately Stephen Cleobury saw it, he said, 'We're doing it.' It was actually performed first at Winchester Cathedral on 22 December 1982, with the King's performance following two days later. This was my first really *popular* piece, I suppose, since *The Whale*. So I came from obscurity back into the public eye again, by way of a very short three-minute carol.

The Lord's Prayer (1982) came to me in a similar way. We had a cottage in Devon at the time and my mother loved driving very fast cars. She drove me all the way home from south Devon to north London in about three and a half hours. During that time I was thinking about the text of the Lord's Prayer and when I got home I went straight to my desk and wrote it out from beginning to end. I wrote *The Lamb* and *The Lord's Prayer* entirely for myself, though I let King's have *The Lamb* for nothing, I so much wanted them to do it. At a later date, in the same way, I made another setting of the Lord's Prayer (1993) in Greek. What really set me free was the fact that I had entered tradition when I wrote the *Orthodox Vigil Service* and so I felt much more confident about what I was doing.

I was now writing with white-hot intensity and at greatly increased speed. I was reading the Fathers and I came across St Simeon the New Theologian, which led me to write *Ikon of Light*.

Ikon of Light (1982) was for me a very important piece. I had met Peter Phillips and there was a great rapport between us, and the sound of the Tallis Scholars had been a great influence on me. Not so much the music they sang, because they sang music of the Renaissance, which is not my favourite period. But the choral music that I wrote during this period was all conceived for the Tallis Scholars.

I had discovered a poem by St Simeon. I was amazed by its imagery and above all by its intensity of light. It was about uncreated light, the light that appeared to Christ on Mount Tabor, the light that shines in saints – you cannot look at them because it's like the light of the sun that actually shines from out of their faces. St Simeon always saw God as uncreated light: all his visions of God were of uncreated light. He wrote his text living in rather obscure voluntary exile in Asia Minor. He was highly critical of what was going on in Constantinople amongst the hierarchy, so it was there in Asia Minor that he wrote these wonderful poems about light. I set one of them, 'Hymn to the Holy Spirit', in Greek, which became the central section of the whole work.

Ikon of Light was a long piece and again it came rather like a lot of these big pieces, in sections. I wrote one section for the Tallis Scholars called *Doxa*, which means glory. *Doxa* then became part of the *Ikon of Light*. And then I wrote another section, very similar to *Doxa*, called 'Fos' ('light'). I was writing for the first time about spiritual states of being.

I started to compose the opening of 'Fos' and I had the idea of a string trio playing in the distance which would represent the soul yearning for God. The choir represented God in his uncreated energies. This yearning chord is played by the string trio which is cut off by the joy/sorrow chord sung by the chorus singing the word 'Fos', light, light, light, light, light, light – until it becomes an expanded light separated from all yet united to all, and it goes straight into the second section, *Doxa*. *Doxa* symbolizes the glory of that light filling everything with light. There follows the traditional Byzantine Hymn sung in Greek: 'Holy God, Holy and strong, Holy and immortal, have mercy upon us.'

The central section is, as I have said, a setting of the poem by St Simeon, a very long section lasting twenty-five minutes. This builds to a huge climax – the music is very silent and very esoteric – 'Come O light, take possession of me, you who are alone come and join me who am also alone.' It's a massive invocation to the Holy Spirit, again sung in Greek and seen through St Simeon's eyes as 'light'.

On either side of this mystic prayer to the Holy Spirit of St Simeon, we have the Byzantine Hymn. The yearning of the soul is always represented by the string trio coming in and out of the *Ikon of Light*. There is also a good deal of use of actual silence, which is another way of showing uncreated light.

The final section mirrors the first, with the word 'Fos' gradually becoming an ocean of uncreated light – an ocean of 'light' where one can swim all one's life. I tried in this last section, and indeed in the whole piece, to create the concept of the uncreated energies of God. 'I cannot look at you, Father, because the light pouring from your eyes blinds me.' So wrote a Russian nobleman while talking to St Seraphim of Sarov, during the last century.

At its première in Tewkesbury Abbey as part of the Cheltenham Festival in the summer of 1984, *Ikon of Light* made quite an impression on a packed audience. An eminent French musicologist referred to it as one of the pillars of sacred music in this century. However, impressive though it was, I was experiencing St Simeon 'second-hand', as it were, and systems still abounded in the music. I had much, much further to go.

Returning to Cecil Collins, I was still desperate to get started on *Mary of Egypt*, and he said, 'Why don't you go and see that old traditionalist rogue, Philip Sherrard? I think he may be the only person who can help you.'

This was a very important time of my life. First of all, my mother had been diagnosed as having cancer, and so I left England not knowing whether she was going to recover. As it happened, she did not, so I left England for Greece not entirely happily but looking forward very much to meeting Philip. I'd heard so much about him from Cecil, some amusing stories, some less flattering. But Cecil said it was quite possible that he might be the only man who could tackle this subject, because, as Cecil said, with a glint in his eye, 'He's very hot on sex and he's very hot on Orthodoxy.'

I arrived in northern Evia, where Philip lived in a converted magnesite mine. It was an amazing place. I remember arriving and going through one of the doors to the property and being greeted by one of Philip's daughters, who took me across to where Philip had his cottage with no electricity – just oil lamps. I thought, so it's here I'm about to meet the man who has translated the *Philokalia*; who has translated modern Greek poetry (of which I knew quite a substantial amount at that time); and who brought into prominence in England poets like Cavafy, Seferis and Sikelianos. It was, in a way, daunting. But as I approached the cottage I heard Wagner. I thought, this is really very odd – what was a traditionalist doing listening to Wagner? It was part of *The Ring*.

Philip totally disarmed me by his charm. Over the week that I was there we had long discussions. It was incredibly stimulating talking to him. He talked about a liturgy of Eros. He said he was nervous about collaborating with a composer, and the only time he'd had any contact with any composer at all was the time when Michael Tippett was composing *The Midsummer Marriage* and had consulted him. Philip had helped him through one fairly major knotty part of the *Marriage*. We talked a lot about possible ways of approaching Mary of Egypt and his first idea was for it to be a liturgy of Eros. He thought there should be two levels existing at the same time – like a liturgy – the heavenly level being mirrored by the earthly level.

I came back to England highly stimulated, thinking, ah yes, yes, he is the man to do it, because of his wonderful ideas and the marvellous way he was able to put things. He had a command of English that allowed him to put across mystical and metaphysical concepts with masterly clarity.

I communicated a good deal with Philip at this period and a lot of the time I talked about my mother and he gave very gentle spiritual counsel. I was extremely depressed, though, when he sent me the first part of the libretto of *Mary of Egypt*, because it began with 'Blessed is the Kingdom of Eros, of the uncreated Eros, for they are of the Kingdom'. It went on in a similarly verbose, abstruse way. I thought, well, nobody's going to know who Mary of Egypt is. There's no communication. It is impressive-sounding metaphysical English; it could be read, but no one will understand a thing. It was totally unsettable to music and was far too complicated. I could see that it would be impossible. It wasn't Philip's fault: I don't think he was capable of writing in the simple way that I discovered was the only way possible way that *Mary of Egypt* could be done.

We went on corresponding with one another. I think it was obvious I was not very enthusiastic and we gradually dropped the subject in our correspondence. But he certainly encouraged me in the artistic direction in which I was going, because he was a traditionalist; he understood exactly what tradition meant – he had spent his life devoted to tradition.

I remember him taking me round various monasteries, and he'd say, 'Write that down; write that down; write that little phrase down; write this little phrase down', which I did. He wasn't particularly musical. I think he just thought – traditionalist that he was – that I had to steep myself in traditional music, in some of the greatest Christian music ever written, which is Byzantine chant. Also he got hold of a Psaltist to sing for me and I noted down a few note patterns. I never made a study of Byzantine chant in an academic way. Egon Wellesz wrote a very long book on Byzantine chant but that gave me very little. You have to live it; you have to listen to it, understand what it's connected to. Go into the desert. Byzantine chant outside the context of the liturgy and outside the context of the meaning of The Word is meaningless. It only becomes meaningful when you see how faithful it is to The Word and how it proclaims The Word.

I brought back to England a notebook full of these little sketches. Sometimes they were only five or six notes; that sort of length. The patterns were totally unconnected to one another because they came from different monasteries. I just jotted down the phrases Philip suggested.

Back in England I discovered that my mother was much worse and that she was going to die. Her death a few weeks later was a very traumatic experience for me, so much so that I decided that I didn't want to write any more music. I went to see Marco Pallis and told him how griefstricken I was and how I didn't want to write any music. He told me to go to the landscape that I loved most and just do nothing, just be totally silent. So I went to Greece and I took with me the fragments I had jotted down on Philip's advice.

While in Greece I went to venerate the relics of St Nektarios of

Pentapolis, the saint who had very recently been canonized by the Orthodox Church. He was a saint to whom I was much drawn, with his love of nature. Although he was quite a learned man, he spent his last years in communion with the pine trees. I put my head on his skull, and I heard the words inside me: 'Where your treasure is, there will your heart be also', which is a quotation from the Gospels and which seemed to give me a tremendous lift. I went back to where I was staying and I pulled out these note patterns – this was after about six weeks of total silence. I started writing. I had with me Philip's book *The Wound of Greece*, also a book of poetry by Andreas Kalvos. I read what Philip had written about Kalvos's poem, *Eis Thanaton* ('To Death'). The poem is about a man who finds himself in a lonely landscape in Greece and he's in despair because he has lost his mother. So, what was to become my *Eis Thanaton* became a monument to my mother and the act of writing it wrote me out of my grief. That's quite an important thing to say: music plays itself within me, takes me out of myself, nourishes me like manna.

Eis Thanaton (1985) is a piece that falls very distinctly into three sections: the son alone in grief, the appearance of his mother, and then the son's resolve to reach the spiritual heights. I was very impressed by what Philip had to say about the whole concept of woman, the whole concept of motherhood, the whole concept of what being a mother is, being ultimately the Mother of God. The text is in Greek and the first section deals with the son's grief, his total despair: trombones, timpani and low strings provide a bleak landscape for the bass voice. Then, from a very high gallery a group of high strings and a soprano enter. It is the voice of his mother. She descends and she sings with all the tenderness of a mother, 'You will not see me for a while, but you must continue, you must continue climbing the spiritual heights.' The last section is the son's determination (after she has vanished) to continue to try and climb the heights. His mother appears and sings, now from a great height, representing the Mother of God. The piece has its basis in Byzantine chant. The

54

last section sounds particularly Byzantine but again there seems to have been some alchemical process which makes the piece sound eternally new. This would sound abominably conceited were I not totally convinced that the music was 'given' to me as a monument of gratitude to my mother, who had given so much to me.

In both *Ikon of Light* and *Eis Thanaton* I was still using systems. I thought I had achieved something in these two pieces, but I still had not rid myself totally of modernism: music-making organized and articulated according to the closed world of 'art for art's sake'. I still found this unsatisfactory; I had to find a way in which to organize and articulate my music according to a different level of reality, beyond music itself.

Take a piece like Beethoven's *Missa Solemnis*, which for me is an absurdity and an anomaly because it resonates only against itself. There is no real prototype in Beethoven's *Missa Solemnis* – he doesn't go back to find the prototype – it's just an excuse for an expansive exercise in anguished self-expression: Beethoven's 'ego' railing against God. As Frithjof Schuon has written, 'There is no denying what is powerful and profound about many of Beethoven's musical motifs, but, all things considered, a music of this sort should not exist; it exteriorises and thereby exhausts possibilities which ought to remain inward and contribute in their own way to the contemplative scope of the soul.' This meant that, for me at least, there were really no mentors among modern composers and I had to seek guidance from someone outside the musical world.

In July of 1986 I met Mother Thekla, Abbess of the Orthodox Monastery of the Dormition at Whitby. She is an amazing woman, a person who seemed to know me almost before I met her. Very quickly she saw the problems that I was having writing music for which I had no contemporary model. She saw that I could not go on doing what I had done so far. We had long discussions about the function of music. If one believes, according to the ancient Taoist philosophy, that music happened at the

Grand Beginning of all things, then, my goodness, as composers we have a mighty responsibility. We cannot just rage with our feeble egos against God. Music has to have some basis in what is ultimately real. A religious picture, however great, is an altogether different thing from a liturgical ikon. One is of this world: it speaks of this world and leaves you in it. In a sense it is not ultimately *real*. The ikon addresses itself to human nature universally, to man's thirst for something beyond. In music it must be the same. For instance, in the Old Testament there is a sacred music for almost every single Hebrew word, pure sacred tradition. So how dare we come along – whoever the composer and however talented, even Stravinsky in his *Abraham and Isaac* – and impose our own ideas on how the thing should be set. It is no longer an ikon in sound.

Of course I'm thinking retrospectively here. It was only much later that I was able to formulate such ideas, which were at the time more or less instinctively felt. Certainly when I went to Mother Thekla I was not clear in my own mind about these ideas.

I had spoken with Mother Thekla on the telephone and had read her book on Mary of Egypt before I met her. Whether there was any possibility of collaboration at that time, I had no idea. After all, she was an abbess in a monastery in Yorkshire and at the same time a highly formidable and beautiful woman in her late seventies, with a ferocious temper and one of the most savage senses of humour I have ever met with. She has the ability never to 'blow the trumpet' of Orthodoxy and to reduce everything to a *terrifying* simplicity: 'None of the churches are even decent now, darling. They probably never were.' She is the most remarkable woman that I have ever met in my life.

We all need a spiritual father. In my case I found a spiritual mother, in Mother Thekla. She might not be right for all people: as I said, she is very formidable, but she has this unique talent for being able to get to the absolute nub of everything. I asked if she would be interested in some kind of collaboration. She answered typically, 'Yes, darling, but behind the scenes.'

With regard to music she is not particularly knowledgeable, not technically knowledgeable. But that didn't matter, because the more she worked with me, the more she understood how I worked and what I needed and how to provide the kind of text that would get me going as well. But this was a long process and I worked with her on many things before tackling *Mary of Egypt*.

In the early period of my talks with Mother Thekla I came across an extraordinary Akathist written by Father Gregory Petrov. An Akathist is a Byzantine term that literally means a service in which you stand throughout – a hymn of thanksgiving, usually in thirteen sections. An Akathist can be addressed to a saint, but the most common form is the Akathist to the Mother of God, which is sung in the Greek Orthodox Church every Friday in Lent. Gregory Petrov was awaiting death in a Siberian labour camp and he took the Byzantine shape of the Akathist to make a kind of personal paean of praise. He took the title of his Akathist from the dying words of St John Chrysostom as he was going to his martyrdom: 'Glory be to God for everything'. And he really meant *everything*, because all suffering comes from God and all joy comes from God – everything comes from God. I remember Mother Thekla at this time saying, 'With this text we must not give a farthing to the Devil.' Of course evil exists but Gregory Petrov managed to sublimate suffering. The text existed, curiously enough, first of all in Italian, then I got a copy of it in Russian and Mother Thekla said that she would translate it into English, and rather typically said she'd improve on it. And she did: it was an amazing text.

This became the *Akathist of Thanksgiving* (1986). One of the wonderful things Mother Thekla used to do, especially in the early days of my collaboration with her, was to have different coloured inks to indicate different things, and she put a kind of metaphysical underlay against almost every sentence of the text where she thought (even if *he* didn't realize it) that Petrov was making a reference to some liturgical event in the Orthodox

Church. This was very exciting for me because for the first time it meant that the music could resonate with the prototype. She put in the margin in green ink, for instance, a certain feast, like the Feast of the Cross, or she would write a reference to the Mother of God, or a reference to the heavenly bridal chamber. So I was given not only a translation but in the margin a metaphysical subtext: she was a thorough Platonist. It was an extraordinary experience to compose the *Akathist*; but when I received the text in this form, I needed to communicate with Mother Thekla every day. I was, after all, treading new territory, where there were so many metaphysical references, almost in every sentence of the piece. I asked Father Michael Fortounatto, 'How can I possibly do this?' And he said, 'Well, you just have to imagine yourself as Adam and tackle it in that way.' Mother Thekla was more 'down to earth'; she said, 'Just get on with it.'

At last I felt I had a much higher level of reality, way beyond the mere technicalities of musical composition to resonate with. I'm not sure whether I thought that at the time but I can say it now with hindsight. My excitement had to do with the fact that even though these metaphysical prototypes existed, there was this odd alchemical change that happened, so it never sounded as if I was copying existing fragments; it sounded as if it had been fully integrated by me and transubstantiated into something 'new' in the sense of Christ's words, 'Behold, I make all things new'. The composition seemed to have little to do with 'me', John Tavener.

The text of the *Akathist of Thanksgiving* is constantly drawing parallels between sensual and spiritual levels of experience: 'How wonderful it is, Lord, when you show us how transient are these pleasures.' It speaks also in great detail about nature and how much that is connected with this divine world. This was a completely new element in my music. There is one particular moment that really comes at the climax of the Akathist. The text makes a reference to the Cross: 'I see your Cross, your Cross for my sake.' Now at that point I slightly misquote an ancient chant that is connected with the Feast of the Cross in the Orthodox

Church. It's sung by a solitary counter-tenor, and then comes the resplendent joy and serenity of 'Now is the triumph of life everlasting', sung and played by all the performers. On the Cross Christ preserves His serene glory, the glory He had with God before the world existed.

Akathist of Thanksgiving was written very quickly but it had to wait a year, until November 1988, for its première in Westminster Abbey. With this new way of writing, I was beginning to find 'The Voice', not *my* voice. I was beginning to extinguish John Tavener. Some other level of reality was taking over. It felt like a wonderful, inspiring take-over. What can I liken it to? It had a certain similarity to what happens when we venerate the relics of a saint. The Fathers say the bones of a saint resonate with the sweet smell of Paradise. So it was a joyful experience; a totally mysterious, inexplicable experience, because of this alchemical change that took place. It was as if I had discovered that I could cooperate with God. It's a relationship. We give back to Him what He has given to us. We provide the bread, He performs the miracle. We provide the wine, He brings about the change. 'God became man because of us, let us become God because of Him.'

Resurrection (1988) began to come to me when I saw the organization of Mother Thekla's texts taken from the Gospels, the Old Testament prophecies and the texts of Orthodox Holy Week. Basically it tells of the Passion and Resurrection of Christ. Symbolism of every kind abounds in this three-and-a-half-hour work. As in *Ultimos Ritos,* all the instruments have symbolic functions and the placing of the singers and instrumentalists is of the greatest importance. For instance, the music of the Evangelist is always the same, although the tones are varied according to the text. The music for Christ becomes the music of Resurrection, but I break this 'convention' altogether in the music of the actual Crucifixion. Christ is 'apparently' alone, Time and Nature are being made new, worldly space is being transfigured. The music at this point owes much to the *dhrupad* style of Indian singing and is used deliberately to 'shock', to become 'frightening', 'incomprehensible'.

I should say at this point that I was inspired to use the *dhrupad* style in my work after hearing the Dagar Brothers sing it. I was deeply moved by its sacredness, its virtuosity, its solemnity. But I have never made a study of it. In so far as I adopt the *dhrupad* style I seek to give only an aural impression of the ancient and sacred style of the Hindustani singing.

In 'My God, My God, why has thou forsaken me?', sung in Aramaic, the range of Christ's voice becomes colossal, bars are being broken, there is no more historical time, but a dynamic liturgical transformation. The howling of the prophets (a separate male voice group with trombone and timpani), that we have heard before, is now gathered up into Christ's voice. Orthodoxy basically sees the Old Testament as a prefiguration of the New. She does not consider it on its own.

The whole of *Resurrection* is framed by 'Paradise', an uncreated music that helps to remove the historical elements – or at least, I hope that history is in a way transfigured. The events in *Resurrection* are not past and dead, but present and active. This is reflected in the music by elements of Judaic, Znamenny, Byzantine chant and magic squares all being synthesized and composed by me to embrace one another, as it were, at the moment of the Resurrection, into a Unity.

After the Crucifixion comes the divine 'chaos', represented in musical terms by the opposite of divine unity – i.e. all the elements of the whole piece run wildly together in ferocious dissonance: bars broken, gates shattered, tombs opened. That same divine power gathers all these elements together in what I hope is a Divine Unity – 'Rise O God and judge the world'. All the musical elements 'embrace' one another when the Evangelist finally disappears from the piece altogether and all the forces that were separate elements sing 'Christ is risen from the Dead' in Greek, English and Church Slavonic. It is as if the music undergoes a change, becoming itself metaphorically (as the Canon of the Resurrection puts it) 'a different way of life'.

This 'different way of life' puzzled modernist critics. They thought I had abandoned art and had even abandoned my duty as a composer. I was to abandon a great deal more. But *Resurrection* was the mightiest undertaking to date and, as with *Ultimos Ritos*, it both closes old doors and opens new ones.

I didn't write it as a commission; nobody asked for it. But when I had completed it, as it happens, a very distant cousin of mine, the conductor and teacher Alan Tavener, rang Chester's saying they wanted a short piece, because Glasgow was going to be the City of Culture that year. So I said, 'Well, it's not short, it's over three hours, but perhaps you would like to hear it?'

I met Alan with his wife at Mother Thekla's monastery in Yorkshire and I played it through on the monastery piano. I played it from beginning to end, singing and playing all the parts. Alan said, 'We've got to do it – we've simply got to do it.' He pulled out all the stops, as it were, and the first performance of what I suppose I now consider to be one of the pieces that is most important to me, was put on in Glasgow Cathedral. It has not been performed anywhere since.

During this period I felt myself groping towards the idea – the *ideal*! – that what I wanted to do was to make ikons in sound. Of course, I never knew whether this would ever be possible. After all, an ikon is a sacred object – it's something that causes an Orthodox to bow his head and then kiss it in veneration. What I loved so much about the ikon was the quality of its tenderness, its serenity, its 'unreality', the fact that unlike Western painting it does not force itself on you in any way. An ikon of the Mother of God holding Christ, or an ikon of Christ himself, seems to say, 'Take me if you want me, leave me if you don't.' It doesn't impose.

One day during 1986 Steven Isserlis rang me up. I had never heard of him; he was apparently a cellist. He said, 'I'm a Jew, I'm a Russian Jew. My father is Russian. I love your music. I particularly love the Russian Orthodox qualities that it has. Although I'm a Jew, I'm not a practising Jew. I always go to the service of

Easter in the Orthodox Church, because I love the music so much and I love the ceremonies. I just wonder whether you could write a piece for cello and orchestra that has some connection with the Orthodox music that I love so much.' Of course, if another kind of cellist had rung me up and said, 'Would you compose a cello concerto?' I would have said, 'No. Absolutely out of the question.' But the way Steven put this question and the fact that he told me he loved Orthodox music somehow excited me. It seemed a genuine way of asking if I would do it.

I rang Mother Thekla immediately, and she said, 'It's a wonderful opportunity, because it could have a metaphysical subject. Find a subject.' And the subject came to me – 'The Protecting Veil'. This is a feast of the Orthodox Church concerning the appearance of the Mother of God in Constantinople when its citizens were being attacked by the Saracen armies. By her presence in the sky, holding a veil over the Christians, the Saracen armies disappeared. I thought this image was wonderful, and that immediately gave me the idea about writing a piece concerning the various feasts of the Mother of God, which was, as it were, my secret metaphysical agenda.

It wasn't necessary for me, as Messiaen had done in a number of his pieces, such as his *Vingt regards sur l'Enfant Jésus*, to write into the score, 'At this moment, this is the Virgin's kiss' and suchlike, as if the music was following a detailed programme. I wasn't interested in proselytizing, I never have been. So far as I was concerned, the subject simply gave me the metaphysical subtext to write the music. The fact that it goes through all the feasts of the Mother of God is of no importance to the listener. What is important to me is the fact that the music has a metaphysical substructure. It's certainly not an abstract title: it means something!

What mattered to me about *The Protecting Veil* (1987) was how I composed it, because I cannot separate composing, the act of working, from prayer. So I noted down all the feasts of the Mother of God; I looked at the various tones that are sung at those feasts. I absorbed them and just started to write an enormously long cello line, from beginning to end, just a monodic arch, with nothing else. And I thought it was extremely beautiful. I then imagined this monodic arch for the cello being played in a building like Agia Sophia in Constantinople, which has a colossal resonance, and I wanted to pick up the resonances of the cello and insert its implied 'horizontal' harmonies. I wanted the string orchestra to pick up these implications. I did not, as composers in the past have done, want to harmonize the melody, or create a counterpoint.

Certain notes resonate in a vast building and imply certain harmonies, certain clusters. I wanted the cello to resonate solely with an orchestra of strings. In a metaphysical way the strings pick up the resonance of the cello, 'undergoing, as it were, the way of negation and not forming ideas about it', as St Gregory Palamas wrote. They have no separate life from the cello.

I wrote *The Protecting Veil* very quickly, because the melodic line came very quickly. When Steven played it through he seemed very happy with it. He made a few suggestions: I'd not written for the solo cello before. He showed me how things might be improved a little if I put them up an octave or down an octave or whatever. Eventually, it was performed at the Proms in September 1989.

At the rehearsals, with the BBC Symphony Orchestra, there was a sort of strange atmosphere because every time these hardened professional players heard it, they applauded. To begin with I thought they were applauding Steven's playing, because it was phenomenal. But then I thought, it can't be just Steven's playing; there must be something about the piece that they like very much. And of course almost overnight that piece became a hit. This took me completely by surprise. There was a lot of fuss, people talking about it in the interval, then on BBC Radio Three. It was as if it had been some sort of revelation.

I received hundreds of letters after that performance. One came from a girl, I imagine in her late teens or early twenties. It was the letter that touched me the most. Because she obviously didn't know what 'The Protecting Veil' was. She said, did I mean by the title that I wanted to protect unfashionable values like beauty and truth? I was very touched. For me the Mother of God is beauty and truth. If this girl interpreted it in another way, that was her business. As Mother Thekla said to me, 'It's none of your business what people say or think. Once it's gone from your study, act *dead*.'

The Protecting Veil was the piece which enabled me to become self-sufficient, and so from the material point of view it was very useful. Steven Isserlis's famous first recording of it with the London Symphony Orchestra took some time to arrange. There was a slightly embarrassing situation because Oliver Knussen had conducted the first performance with the BBC Symphony Orchestra. It took some time to establish why Steven should record it with the London Symphony Orchestra. I also wanted to use Gennady Rozhdestvensky, because of all the conductors of the music which I'd been writing around this period, he seemed to be the most sympathetic. He is also Orthodox and therefore able to draw something more out of the music. In the end Virgin decided to record it with the LSO in Maida Vale studios.

The recording went very well. Typical of Gennady, he came in and he said, 'Darling! Darling, it's so wonderful, it's so beautiful, but where are the winds?' I said, 'There aren't any.' 'Where are the brass?' I said, 'There aren't any.' He said, 'But, my dear, it's so beautiful – I love it.'

'I'M JUST A PIECE OF MUSIC'

Soon after finishing *The Protecting Veil*, I wrote a string quartet – *The Hidden Treasure* (1989). Cecil Collins had long wanted me to write a string quartet, so had my godmother, and so did the other nun with Mother Thekla. Mother Katherine had just died of cancer and another dear friend had been killed in Greece, so I thought I might write a very intimate and contemplative quartet in their memory.

The Hidden Treasure has nothing to do with the classical Western string quartet – mine stands still, but with occasional outbursts. It also has a metaphysical subtext which is taken from the three-hour-long *Resurrection*. Somehow I had to distil and mirror the larger work, but also create something quite different. Although it is based on *Resurrection,* it inhabits a totally different world. The music sighs, breaks the heart and reveals itself in tears, cries and gestures. The drama of *Resurrection* has been punctured. The massive has become small, with only four instruments. The grandeur has gone. It is like a miniature which reflects, ponders on and contemplates aspects of the Passion and Resurrection. It is never dramatic – it is ecstatically unmoving. It is like a tiny ikon of the Resurrection. In some ways it goes deeper, because it is only concerned with the essentials. In each part, in each fragment, the mystery of the whole is found. Although it is a reflection of something else, it seems new and heard for the first time.

In the final section there is an unspoken tribute to Beethoven and to Mother Katherine, who listened (while she was dying) to nothing but the quartet which Beethoven wrote in thanksgiving for his return to health. But this too is only an essence. It has nothing to do with Beethoven's world. *The Hidden Treasure* has already gone somewhere else: not better, just somewhere else.

In all this time I still had not found the right librettist for *Mary of Egypt*. The difficulties remained: the mixture of her early life of being a prostitute and then the last part of her life being a sort of desert mother living in the harsh extreme of the desert wilderness. But I was determined to find the proper language and way of doing it, even though it seemed at times I never would. During the summer of 1989 I returned to work on this long-nurtured project.

I went to Mother Thekla and asked her to 'Listen to Stravinsky's *Les Noces*, listen to *The Magic Flute* and think about Noh drama and those wonderful naïve Coptic ikons. I think that *Mary of Egypt* comes somewhere in there, if that makes sense to you.' She listened to *The Magic Flute* and to *Les Noces*, and then she wrote her first rough draft for *Mary of Egypt* (completed 1989) and sent it to me. I rejected it. I said, 'It's not simple enough, it's not pared down enough, it's still too complicated.' Then she sent a second one; I rejected that – I said, 'It's still not simple enough.' Then I rejected the third one – I said, 'It's not simple enough.' The fourth one . . . and then the fifth one came and she said, 'This is it, I'm not doing another one.' This last was absolutely perfect, because it had what I was really looking for – though I didn't know it at the time. This enabled me to cope with the sexuality, not in a contemporary way but in a very stylized, very childlike way – the way a child would understand it. This is exactly what, in the end, Mother Thekla's libretto provided. She said, 'Now, it's the music that has got to do it. I have just given you the raw material.'

Mother Thekla had no time whatsoever for opera as such. In any case we had fairly early on decided that we did not want anything like a conventional opera. I had asked her to listen to *Les Noces* and *The Magic Flute*, which she loved, but they are very cerebral and sophisticated pieces, after all. *Les Noces*, it is true, is a very folky piece, but Stravinsky is always sophisticated – he couldn't help it, that was the kind of composer he was. And *The Magic Flute* is sophisticated, although it has childlike qualities. But *Mary of Egypt* is much less sophisticated because of its subject: it's more raw and far more like those wonderful Coptic ikons.

Again, I had no precedent to work from. Not even with, for instance, Britten's Church Parables. I feel they start off in a marvellous way, with monks coming in singing plainsong, but then after about five or ten minutes you're back to subjective Britten again. I like the way they were staged but somehow, for me, they do not remain objective. To my ears the composer's personal obsessions return all too soon and his twentieth-century humanism jars horribly with the objectivity of plainsong.

I didn't want anything operatic, anything of the conventions for expressing all-too-human passions and feelings. I didn't know many Noh plays but I had seen some and I had watched very stylized Indian dancing, and this is the way I wanted *Mary* to look. I knew that right from the time I received the final libretto.

We decided to call it a moving ikon rather than an opera. Others might have had a field day with Mary's prostitution, but we tried to integrate the two halves of her life. Mother Thekla had always said (and this had already impressed me in her book) that Mary's prostitution was only the other side of the coin. It was *love* because she would never take money. But, she added, it was probably a misdirected love, and it was only when she went out into the desert that this love became a true love, a free love. At last she had somewhere to channel this enormous love that she had in her.

I had slight reservations about the production of *Mary of Egypt* at the Snape Maltings Concert Hall near Aldeburgh – not so much the production as the set designs. I felt that modernism had crept in. It cost a lot of money to build the set and yet it looked to me like an aircraft hangar. Also I think the desert monks should have been shown as Byzantine ikonic figures rather than as something like those Hare Krishna people you see wandering along Oxford Street ringing bells and dressed in saffron robes. It could all have been much simpler. But the critics seemed to love it and Bishop Kallistos, who was sitting next to me, said, 'Well, John, Mary of Egypt will never be the same for me again. Both you and Mother Thekla have got it *absolutely right*.'

Some time way before the première of *Mary of Egypt*, I had been in Greece for a couple of months, during the autumn of 1990. Basically to work, but also to relax. Music was coming to me now at lightning speed: I was composing, composing and composing, I was writing obsessively – I couldn't stop. In fact, when the sun went down, I just worked and worked through the night. I probably didn't do myself much good, working in a sedentary position for excessively long periods of time. I was writing *We Shall See Him As He Is* (1990) for Richard Hickox.

I was also writing an enormous amount of unaccompanied

choral music. Richard Steinitz has said that I have written more unaccompanied choral music than Britten, and more than any English composer for a very long time.

When I was writing *We Shall See Him As He Is*, lots of other ideas, sort of chips off the block, if you like, came to me: unaccompanied choral pieces. Somebody very close to me had died and I wrote a piece for unaccompanied cello. Greece, from this time onwards, appeared to stimulate me to write very quickly. As time moved from October into November in 1990, the days got shorter and shorter and so I used all the daylight hours to write music. By the end of this period, and this must have been about late November, I had a huge pile of manuscripts: the completed *We Shall See Him As He Is*, the completed *Thrinos* (1990), an unaccompanied cello piece, and several completed unaccompanied choral pieces. I was carrying around a huge amount of music.

I recall I went to some of the old haunts that I used to go to when I was much younger, when I first got to know Greece – places like Glifada, Vouliagmeni by the sea. I ought to have been feeling very pleased with myself because I'd written so much. I was pleased with the music and yet I felt this underlying depression, the kind of depression I had when I was eighteen, nineteen, twenty, those sort of years. I was wandering around, very much on my own, muttering to myself, 'I want to die, I want to die, I want to die.' Then I thought: why am I doing this? I've written all this music and yet I'm wandering round muttering these things. I had noticed that my heart had been thumping a great deal, especially when I was in bed at night. Eventually I rang my brother from Athens and I said, 'My heart is thumping very loudly and I just wonder, do you think I ought to see someone?' He said, 'For God's sake, absolutely, yes.'

Just before I came back from Greece, I remember making perhaps the most extreme prayer that I'd ever made in my life. Although I was writing music, I wasn't married, I was still living with my father, which is unusual in a way and it was beginning to bother me. My father was getting older and I just did not see any particular future beyond the fact that I was writing music. I made a prayer to the Mother of God: 'Do with me whatever you want. If you want death, I'm ready.' I don't think I was ready. 'If you want me to continue, then I will continue.' It was strange that I made that prayer, not knowing then that I needed major heart surgery.

When I got back to England in the late November of 1990, it was clear that I needed immediate heart surgery. But it couldn't be done straight away because of a suspected malignant tumour in the bottom of my jaw. I had to have that removed first. But all during this time, even when I was in hospital, I couldn't stop writing. I knew that I could die during the heart operation and that this might be the end of everything.

I was getting weaker and weaker all the time, because my heart was becoming worse and worse. But I had to wait until the operation on my jaw had completely healed. During this period of about three months I managed to sketch out *The Apocalypse* (1991–2) in rather faint pencil. Had I died I wonder if anybody would have been able to transcribe the piece. But at least I had the satisfaction of knowing that I had written it. I finally had the heart surgery in April 1991.

Mother Thekla had provided a most intricate libretto which had more metaphysical subtexts than anything she had ever written before. There were arrows going this way and that, connections being made from this to that – there wasn't a thing in *The Apocalypse* (not a note, not a rhythm, not a harmony) that, when I finally completed it, could not be explained metaphysically. Everything, but everything, was both metaphysically and musically related. Whether you could say that this was another kind of 'sacred chant' I cannot say. But I know that the final achievement of *The Apocalypse* has not yet been realized.

Many people greet me in airport lounges saying, 'Oh, Mr Tavener, that *Apocalypse*, I'm speechless' – or words to that effect. One critic, Paul Driver, seemed to realize its 'importance' and its 'numinous quality' (his words). I am very rarely grateful to a critic, but I was impressed that he could break down his modernist preoccupations and just *react*. I am also grateful for the vast numbers of the public who have said how much *The Apocalypse* has meant to them.

I also wrote a second String Quartet during this period, immediately after I had finished *The Apocalypse*. This quartet had its connections with *The Apocalypse* in the way that *The Hidden Treasure* has connections with *The Resurrection*. *The Last Sleep of the Virgin* (1991), as it's called, was written for almost inaudible string quartet and bells. I think this inaudibility reflected my curious spiritual and physical state at the time. I was so weak and was on the threshold of life and death. My future wife, Maryanna, became my helpmate and tended me daily.

Mother Thekla, wisely as I now see, said, since the Quartet was to do with the Dormition of the Mother of God, I ought to write just a few notes of another piece that I was thinking of writing. This was like a new possibility to return to. So, in a totally exhausted state – I had finished, in faint pencil, *The Apocalypse* and *The Last Sleep of the Virgin* (in barely legible sketches) – I wrote just the first few notes of a piece that might or might not happen.

During the writing of *The Last Sleep of the Virgin*, as I have said, I was in a very strange state. First of all I was extremely weak. It was difficult for me even to get across the room to go to the toilet. In this state, in bed, I went on writing. It remains a bit of a mystery to me where the notes came from. Perhaps they were 'given' to me because death was staring me straight in the face; but I was too weak to comprehend even that. For the first time in my life I really did not quite know, or care very much, where the music was coming from. I just felt the enormous need to get it down on paper. Even now I find it difficult to listen to *Last Sleep*. It's a very strange piece, quite dissonant, and it still sounds obscure to me. Not that obscurity is a bad thing in itself. Complexity is another matter. Certainly when you're talking in traditional terms, complexity represents evil.

*

The few notes that Mother Thekla advised me to get down on paper became the beginning of *Let's Begin Again* (1991–4). This was, in a way, an extroverted version of *The Dormition of the Mother of God*. It was a theatrical piece that I wanted to write for children. After about the fourth week in hospital, having survived the operation, I began to hear those notes again. I wanted manuscript paper but nobody would allow me to have any. When I finally went home after several weeks, and still in a very weak state, I went to the piano and played those few notes. So the piece started to take shape. There was an ambient electronic hum in Harefield Hospital and since I think nothing happens by accident I made this hum the *ison* or eternity note.

Let's Begin Again is quite vigorous music, quite Greek or Middle Eastern in its character. I thought I was writing it for children, but when I started noting the score down I realized it needed adults to sing it, even though I still wanted children to mime the enactment of the Falling Asleep of the Mother of God. It was a kind of thanksgiving for my return to health. The Mother of God had indeed answered my awesome prayer.

One of the performances of *Let's Begin Again* was at a marvellous festival of the sacred in Paris; they had Sufi players, Indian music, Byzantine music as well as music of the American Indians. This festival ran from about November until Christmas Day. I thought it was a wonderful idea, having a festival of sacred music. But the very first performance was in Norwich Cathedral: the second was at Greenwich; then it was done in Paris, where it was translated into French. But I retain a particularly fond memory of the première in Norwich, because children were used for miming and Lucy Bailey's production was 'artless' in the best sense.

After the Paris performance in November 1996 a lot of younger composers came to talk to me. They said there was a big thing going on in France now: modernism was finished, Boulez was finished, he was a wonderful conductor of certain music but his kind of music was not wanted any more. I cannot say whether this was the general view at the time, but the young people I spoke to seemed to be very much in sympathy with what I was doing, and also in sympathy with composers like Arvo Pärt.

Perhaps the French have always had some sense of the sacred, otherwise people like René Guénon and Henri Corbin could not have existed in France. The younger generation of French people, particularly the composers and artists I spoke to in Paris, had a great feeling for this. There's hardly a single educated Frenchman who has not heard of Guénon. As far as a sense of tradition is concerned, perhaps it has existed in France in a way it probably has not existed in England. The younger composers who are coming along, those who don't want to work in the avant-garde intellectual kitchens of modernism, are far more interested in the concept of the sacred. They read people like Guénon, in particular *La crise du monde moderne*, which should be read by every composer, artist and critic before they do anything else – *certainly* before they cast a glance in the direction of modernism.

I returned to texts by Akhmatova in *Akhmatova Songs* (1992), a very different kind of piece from the earlier *Akhmatova Requiem*. These songs are all short poems written at different periods in her life. I asked Mother Thekla to translate them all, although I set them in Russian. I was very attracted to their simplicity, their starkness, their lack of frills, their complete lack of complexity. We put them together as a sort of cycle, and I wrote the setting for two artists I so much admired and was working a good deal with – Steven Isserlis and Patricia Rozario, the Indian singer to whom they are dedicated. I love these songs, they are among my favourite pieces. I love their simplicity, I love their ethos. One is based on an Indian raga, although I don't think anybody would know that, listening to it. After their first performance the critic Andrew Porter said they were 'desperately undercomposed'. Undercomposed for whom? What did he want me to do? Add a figured base? I made another version of them for String Quartet, because the Chilingirian Quartet wanted to do something for voice and quartet, so I thought to arrange these pieces would be a very good idea. However, I prefer the version for solo cello and voice.

I also completed in 1992 *Hymns of Paradise*. These were settings for bass solo, boys' voices and six violins, of poems by St Ephrem, the Syrian. I had discovered him when I set *Thunder Entered Her* (1990) two years earlier.

St Ephrem is perhaps the greatest poet of the Patristic age. His poems abound in strong metaphors and imagery. I scored them for just treble voices and high strings. Ephrem speaks about Paradise in the most vivid and wonderfully naïve way; about cripples leaping around, flying through the air, about those who had never spoken spontaneously singing, those who had never heard suddenly hearing the choirs of angels – absolutely marvellous stuff. The music just flowed out of me.

As to what I feel I was achieving in works of this period, I think human emotion seems to have gone; something else has taken over. It's as if composing with the human mind has all but disappeared. There is a feeling in these pieces that I'm beginning to approach the Platonic ideal of not composing with my personal voice but through some higher agency.

A critic wrote about them that I was not fulfilling my duty as a composer. I was very pleased indeed to read that. For a composer to labour over a score for years and years is incomprehensible to me. During this period and right up till now, if I have to labour with something for more than an hour I dismiss it as not being worthy of attention – not for me as the composer and therefore probably not for the listener. The concept, from both a Christian and Platonic point of view, is that all music already exists. When God created the world he created everything. It's up to us as artists to find that music. Of course that's an exhausting experience, but you have to rid yourself of any preconceived idea about what music is; rid yourself of the idea that you *have* to struggle over note rows, or with sonata form, or the humanist bugbear, development. Music just is. It exists. If you have ears to hear, you'll hear it!

Certainly the short choral pieces and the short unaccompanied pieces for cello come fully born, as did *Song for Athene* in 1993.

Athene was a young girl whom I never actually met, though members of my family knew her. She was tragically killed in a cycling accident, and I went to her funeral in the Russian Orthodox cathedral. This was an extraordinary day. I found, when I'd come away from the burial, there already existed in my mind a piece in memory of her. The notes existed; I had not yet found the words. I rang Mother Thekla that same day and I said, 'I want words. The sound has come to me but I can't find the words.' The next day in the post, believe it or not, came the text taken from *Hamlet* – 'May flights of angels sing thee to thy rest' – and verses taken from the Orthodox funeral service with very gentle alleluias in between. Although it was retitled for the occasion, *Song for Athene* went on to become the music that was played when the coffin of Diana, Princess of Wales, was carried out of Westminster Abbey.

Some time during 1992 Yuri Bashmet, the Russian viola player, asked me to write a piece for him. I presumed he had heard something like *The Protecting Veil*. The London Symphony Orchestra also wanted me to write a piece. So I wrote *The Myrrh-Bearer* (1993) for Yuri. But I didn't want to follow on the example of *The Protecting Veil* – I didn't want to use the orchestra. I chose instead to use the LSO chorus. And, as always, the music had a metaphysical subtext; in this case I was inspired by the great Troparion (a Byzantine verse form) of Cassiane, which is sung in Holy Week in the Orthodox Church. I wanted the viola line to reflect the actual words – almost line by line but without any words – of this marvellous text of the Troparion, 'I who have fallen into many sins.'

Cassiane was supposed to have been mistress to a Byzantine emperor, even when she became a nun. Anyway, this great

Troparion was coming totally from deep, deep within her. She was undergoing prayer of the deepest repentance, and in the contemplation which follows prayer (as St Gregory of Nyssa says), the intellect goes beyond prayer and with the discovery of a higher state prayer is left behind. Then the intellect does not pray with prayer, but attains ecstasy among things which are incomprehensible and lie beyond the world of mortals, and it falls silent in its ignorance of everything of this world. This is the ignorance which is higher than knowledge.

This is what I wanted the viola line to mirror. It starts on its lowest note and throughout the piece climbs, with more and more ecstatic power and with anarchic, worldly interruptions (written by Mother Thekla) for the chorus and bass drums. Then, at the end, the viola, representing Mary Magdalene, metaphorically falls at the feet of Christ in recognition of his divinity. So, in a sense, the viola – Mary Magdalene – Cassiane – attains a new form of perception, and they see and in the viola music all worldly constructions disappear, as things which will sooner or later 'grow old like a garment'. At least, that is what I intended.

The chorus and the bass drum somewhat shockingly represent worldly knowledge, which can only see things from a human point of view and is mechanical, mindless and sterile right up to and including the shattering final statement – 'We have no king but Caesar – Caesar – Caesar!' This is the ultimate denial of God and could well apply to the horrifying mass genocide that is taking place in our world today – well on the way to total ruin. But through the world of corruption (chorus and bass drum), the viola rises to a joyful and uncreated light which reveals the true meaning of creation: 'the inner essences of created things', as St Maximus the Confessor puts it.

I had reservations about the first performance of *The Myrrh-Bearer*. First of all, it was performed in the wrong environment – in the Barbican Concert Hall. Also, if my Russian had been more fluent, I might have been able to communicate more clearly the metaphysical subtext to Yuri. Later, I heard a performance from Liverpool Cathedral, with an unknown young viola player, and I was completely shattered by it. I have never written anything quite like *The Myrrh-Bearer* but I still await the truly authentic performance.

The Greek word '*agraphon*' means 'unwritten saying'. It is also the title of a poem by the modern Greek poet Angelos Sikelianos, which had originally been drawn to my attention during a Temenos Conference at Dartington Hall in 1988. *Agraphon* (1995) is a setting of the poem for solo soprano, strings and two sets of chromatic timpani. It was commissioned by the Athens Festival and performed in the amazing Megaron – the only concert hall I would not like to blow up.

They had asked for a twenty-minute piece for voice and orchestra, and since Patricia Rozario was involved in *The Apocalypse*, which was also being performed at this festival, I decided to set the poem for her voice. I first of all went back to the original Greek, as I often set things in Greek. But I found the English translation by Philip Sherrard so wonderful and it meant a great deal to me. I was moved to tears at the rehearsals – and I was not alone in this. There were intelligent Greek friends in the audience, who found themselves unable to speak after the performance. Why I feel very happy about it, and why I love it so much, is because the music, although put together by me, is entirely, absolutely entirely, formed by traditional means.

The poem describes Christ and his disciples walking outside the city of Zion and they come to a rubbish dump, the kind of rubbish dump you see outside any Greek or Middle Eastern town. And lying on the top of this dump is the carcass of a dead dog. The disciples say to Christ, 'Rabbi, how can you bear to stand here with this terrible stench?' And his answer is, 'If you are pure inside you will not smell the stench.' And Sikelianos rather movingly connects it to Athens during the German occupation. The first half of the poem talks about Christ and his disciples, and the way they cup their noses because of the stench. In the second half of the poem, very strikingly, Sikelianos puts the words into his own mouth and says, 'And now Lord, I, the least of men, stand before You. Give me something of Your holy calm as I walk through this terrible stench.'

Going back to the music, which is inseparable from the words anyway, I represent the calm of Christ by a Byzantine tone. The notion of 'naked putrefaction', which is coming from the rubbish dump, is symbolized by a descending series of dominant sevenths going into hellish regions, with double flats, but actually being transcended at the same time by the presence of Christ. Everything in the poem and the music is transcended. God is present, but in the midst of apparent naked putrefaction.

These dominant sevenths spiralling down to hellish realms represent 'naked putrefaction' – the carcass of the dead dog, the rubbish dump. I used a sacred technique, something of the manner of the *dhrupad*, the great sacred Indian chant, in order to represent the wildly spiralling vocal line that speaks 'the hope of the eternal'. I wondered, however, if even Patricia would ever be able to sing it, because it demands well-nigh impossible singing of microtones, sung in *dhrupad* style, but with a range beyond almost any singer. This symbolized the carcass and the 'lightning flash, the pledge of the eternal'. Also, I wanted to get in a 'double movement' of Christ saying that this is something very beautiful, the dead dog and the stench, because the real 'stench' was back in the city of Zion. In the poem the disciples were not up to seeing that, they could only smell the naked stench and see the unpleasant sight of the carcass of a dead dog. In this fierce and dramatic piece, where there is a Byzantine melodic line together with ever-falling dominant sevenths and very fast microtonal Indian spiralling, it was almost impossible to notate the voice part. Indeed, I had to invent a notation indicating the degrees of microtonal inflection and another to denote the wild and possessed microtonal spiralling of the soprano voice. The strings of the orchestra remain 'frozen' throughout in a sound of petrified ecstasy; the timpani roll and give sudden 'Greek' hammer-blows of fate.

The Indians believe that there are *eight* microtones between a semitone, which means that you have to have an ear of phenomenal acuteness to be aware of which of the eight microtones it is. Western music only concerns itself with white notes and black notes and is, therefore, terribly limited. The Indian belief (and I'm absolutely sure they are right, because I've heard them singing it) means that they can hear eight microtones in between the black and white notes of a piano keyboard. The Byzantines believe there are only four microtones. I was trying to express these different degrees of microtonal inflection in music that moves very fast. There are *dhrupad*-like sudden splurges of notes going up and up at great speed and Patricia has to somehow be in between the notes microtonally all the time. She was helped by the fact that the strings sometimes provide notes. Stringed instruments can more easily find the correct microtone out of the eight microtones in between the semitones than a Western-trained singer.

Agraphon is a work that I love more than any other. It comes out not sounding Byzantine, not sounding particularly Indian: it comes out like an unbridled, possessed, gentle, lyrical thunderbolt, and this pleased me greatly. The very opening of *Agraphon* and the very end are based on the harmonic series which is connected with the music of the spheres, which in turn is connected to the endless song of the angels. Everything in the piece has a traditional significance.

It's not a long piece and I can only presume that the reason it causes people (including myself) to cry is partly because of all the dramatic changes that occur in it. Also, more important, I think, is the fact that the music has been plucked out, as it were, from something that has always existed and which touches the primordial part of us; 'the intellective organ of the heart' is awakened. Eastern music has always understood this. I cannot think of any Western composer, unless it be Hildegard von Bingen, who has written with the intellective organ of the heart.

When I told Mother Thekla that I wanted to write a piece of

music about the afterlife, she nearly fell over flat! She said, 'Now you *seriously* want me to write a piece about the afterlife. What next, for heaven's sake?' I had read a book by Father Seraphim Rose, who was a Californian monk and hermit. He had written a very long book called *The Toll Houses*, and I sent it to Mother Thekla. She said, 'First of all, I don't know what the Toll Houses are' (and very many Orthodox don't know). In any case, she took a very dim view of them because she didn't believe in the idea that anybody could know so precisely what was going to happen after death. 'It sounds like London Airport to me – if you've done this, you're sent here; if you've done that, you're sent somewhere else.' That did not go with her Platonic way of thinking.

There was a silence which lasted quite some time, then eventually she did send a libretto and I must say when I first looked at it I thought: maybe she's going a bit dotty. This is a bit like a Whitehall farce, but full of irony. She said she had to get it out of her system because she so detested the concept of the Toll Houses from a literal point of view. This was the first time for a long time that irony had come my way.

I quickly concluded that as it stood I could not set the libretto to music. In the meantime we talked a lot about the unbelievable dullness of sinful behaviour. I thought that was a marvellous way of putting it across. Eventually, after looking at this libretto for a long time I rang her up and I said, 'Look, it doesn't resonate against anything.' She said, 'Well, I'm sorry, but I don't believe in the Toll Houses.' I responded, 'Yes, but symbolically I can well believe in them, even if half of me hasn't got a clue what happens after death. The saints have dreamed and had visions of the Toll Houses so they cannot be totally ridiculous.' I also explained that I had to use liturgical texts so that the music could resonate against something metaphysical, because the libretto is deeply imaginative but there's nothing metaphysical in it. I then asked her, 'Can I use various texts at certain points taken from Orthodox services?' and she said, 'No! *Absolutely* no!' However, when I rang her up the next day and said, 'Unless I can use a liturgical text, I can't do this piece,' she said, 'Of course you can use liturgical texts. Did I ever say you couldn't? My dear, you can do whatever you like.' *The Toll Houses* was completed in 1996.

Just as *The Hidden Treasure* grew out of *The Resurrection*, so my third Quartet, *Diódia*, grew out of *The Toll Houses*.

Diódia (1995) is liquid metaphysics. It is distilled from *The Toll Houses* but it is wordless and more 'silent'. It is also very long. But I am no longer concerned with such matters. I am not writing music that answers to the hypersensitive critical faculties of listeners (critics or otherwise) that might or might not be bored by repetitions. *I do not care!* In a way I feel released from care. *Diódia* is the length it is because that is its length. The music is not clever; whether it is profound, I cannot say . . .

The Irish audience at Bantry House in Western Cork seemed to find it moving, other-worldly and mysterious, but they were disturbed by the endless knocking of the wood on the viola, expressing in Sufi terms the heartbeat. The music is basically frozen and the worldly outbursts are to me like phantoms of things in the past. When the knocking finally ceases, the viola player sings very, very quietly, 'God, O God, O God, O God.' To me it is music written at the 'end point' – neither here nor there – a music of 'not knowing'; what Plato refers to as the *double ignorance*.

Diódia should be played in a church or in a sacred space, with subdued lighting. It is not music for dissection, therefore it should not even be played in a concert hall. I am thinking of those wonderful concerts in India where people come in and go out while the music is in progress. But it's not quite like that either. Critics should be banned, unless they want to forget the world and simply contemplate.

In 1996 I wrote a piece posthumously dedicated to Philip Sherrard: *Wake Up and Die*. It's for solo cello and the cello section of the orchestra. The metaphysical basis of the piece is the idea which we find in mystics of all traditions, that of dying to your empirical self, your lesser self, your egotistical self, in order to wake up to your eternal self.

The story of its origin is rather curious, though it would not seem so to a holy man or to a monk. Philip Sherrard was, as I understood from his daughter, very ill – I didn't know that he was actually dying. I don't think even she knew at the time. He'd been taken to a hospital in London and I was flying back from Greece, hopefully to see him, when an extraordinary thing happened. We had been airborne for about half an hour when suddenly there came over me a feeling of intense joy, an ecstasy almost, that I had never known before. My last relations with Philip had been less than cordial – in connection with personal matters – yet I loved him very much. In fact, next to my father, maybe he was one of the men I loved most. I wasn't particularly thinking about him, though I was hoping that I might see him in London. Suddenly at two o'clock, which was twelve o'clock English time, this extraordinary feeling, almost of ecstatic forgiveness, came over me. As I later learned, Philip had died at exactly this time. I started singing and I felt as if I was drunk without wine. A melody came to me, which became the beginning of *Wake Up and Die*. The melody was the opening chant-like passage which was played on the cello. I composed the whole piece when I got back to England. I relate this story simply because it is an example of music being given to me in a way that I'd never experienced. The death of people has very often produced music in me, but not in quite this extraordinary way. I can only refer to it as a kind of mystical experience.

Vlepondas (1996), which means 'sight', was commissioned by the Cultural Centre in Delphi, who had asked for a piece connected with ancient Greek drama. Here I had the opportunity to use Patricia Rozario and the legendary Spiros Sakkas, the Greek baritone – who can sing incredibly high and incredibly low notes – and a cellist. As usual it was very important for me to know what the subject was, and I found it difficult to set Greek drama on its own because I find it so merciless, as in a way the landscape

around Delphi is merciless. It needed a kind of Christian counterpart because as the Old Testament connects to the New, so
does the ancient Hellenic world. I told Mother Thekla about this
and she provided, very quickly as usual, a short text which dealt
with the blinding of Oedipus, the earthly king who, when
blinded, begins to 'see'. The text contrasts this with the blind
beggar who came to Christ to ask to receive sight. He was blind
and he received sight. So there are the two kinds of seeing. When
we think we can see with our physical eyes, we are often blind
spiritually. Then there is the worldly acclaimed King Oedipus,
set against the true kingship of Christ God, murdered and
despised by the world. The point is, we have to become blinded
to the world. The beggar saw because he saw Christ and because
he saw God. Oedipus only saw spiritually when he could see no
more with his physical eyes.

Over the years I have grown to want to hear my music performed in venues other than the usual clinical acoustic space of
the modern concert hall. The performance at Delphi gave me an
opportunity to hear *Vlepondas* performed in a sacred space
other than that of an English cathedral. It has been performed in
concert halls since but it didn't resonate with the 'ages of ages',
as it were; when it was performed in the Festival Hall, for
instance. By contrast, under the stars at night the music res-
onated against the ancient amphitheatre of Delphi. It seemed to
be part of life, you could see the stars, you didn't have to look at
ugly lights.

This was not the only piece that was performed in a sacred
space. I also conducted part of *The Apocalypse* in the ancient
amphitheatre at Ephesus. That was a most memorable occasion,
not because the acoustics were so vibrant, as they might have
been in a Western cathedral, but because of the fact that St Paul
had preached at Ephesus. It meant that the music was being performed, literally, in a *temenos*. If we conceive of sacred things,
they have to be worthy of the sacred, therefore they must be performed in sacred spaces. The modern concert hall attempts to be
a purely secular space: an anomaly.

Prince Charles has become a personal friend and also a kindred spirit. That is why I decided to dedicate *Fall and Resurrection* to him, and also to my father's memory. *Fall and Resurrection* (1996–7) deals with the beginning of the world, even before the beginning of the world as a physical creation. I don't believe in the 'bugbear' of evolution. I believe in the Genesis account of the beginning of the world. Its origin is in an uncreated state before there is anything at all, then after the 'uncreated chaos' God loves the world into being; then the Paradise and the Fall, right up to the Resurrection of Christ and of the whole cosmos. After that it is up to us.

I remember feeling very confident with this piece that I was working within tradition. At the start there is the representation of chaos, uncreated chaos, where God is still present but none the less there is chaos – it is not given to us to know what this chaos is. I decided the only way I could do this was to create a music that was constructed and yet was enormously compli-cated; so fast, so slow and so dense, so dissonant that it is all but impossible to hear what is going on. In fact, you could say that I used a modernist technique in order to represent metaphysically this state of chaos. Were anyone simply to hear the opening of *Fall and Resurrection* out of context they could well be mistaken for thinking they were hearing music of the 'new complexity'. Now out of this complexity comes a single note which becomes the *ison*, the eternity note of God held very softly by the double basses – then we hear the first sound of Paradise, played on the Persian *nāy*. The composition of this 'chaos' was a nightmare for me – I loathed doing it. It took me about six weeks to compose one page, and I had to cover fourteen pages, so that's six times fourteen. I've never had to work so hard in all my life.

Fall and Resurrection is to be given its world première in St Paul's Cathedral on 4 January 2000.

Petra (1996) was written for the Gogmagogs, at the request of their founder and producer Lucy Bailey. This group of superb string players can do extraordinary choreographic things like standing on their heads, crawling around and still play like angels. *Petra* is based largely on poetry by the Greek poet Seferis and once I saw the text I just wrote it. It was a spontaneous reaction to fragments of poetry from Seferis.

... *Depart in Peace* ... (1997) came to me almost fully grown, after my father had died – the man I was closest to in the world. The text is taken from the song of St Simeon – 'Lord now lettest thou thy servant depart in peace'. It lasts over twenty minutes and is written for Patricia Rozario, Indian tampura and strings. It came to me complete, which has never happened before with a work of such length.

Eternity's Sunrise (1997) was inspired by two sections of poems by William Blake: a section that deals with seeing eternity in an hour, then 'he who kisses the joy as it flies lives in eternity's sunrise'. This was an important piece in so far as I was asked by the conductor of the Academy of Ancient Music, Paul Goodwin, to write for baroque strings, baroque flute, baroque oboe, lute and handbells. I hope this is the beginning of a real collaboration with the Academy of Ancient Music. When I first heard *Eternity's Sunrise* I was quite taken aback by the sound of it – the much more sober, transparent and ancient sound of the baroque instruments. I much prefer these to the rather brash sound of the modern symphony orchestra. Again, *Eternity's Sunrise* came to me almost fully grown, in the same way that *Depart in Peace* had come. Perhaps my reaction to the sound of it had something to do with the fact that these earlier instruments, with their less assertive timbres, themselves suggest a more hieratic approach to music-making.

After *Eternity's Sunrise* came a very strange experience in my life. As a family we decided to go to Greece for six months to live in our house in Evia. I had been reading a text by St Dionysios the Areopagite, and it refers to the Trinity and the oneness of the Trinity. I had been commissioned by the London Schools' Symphony Orchestra to write a piece and I imagine they expected me to write something like Britten's *A Young Person's Guide to the Orchestra*, or a sort of Bartók *Concerto for Orchestra*. In the event I had no control over what I wrote. Something seemed to take over from outside.

Quite early on I decided the orchestra should to be split into three sections, rather like the ikon of the Trinity painted by Andrei Rublev which depicts God the Father in the middle, God the Son and God the Holy Spirit on either side, both looking towards God the Father. When I arrived in Greece I began to write, but I simply cannot say where the music came from. I should point out that we are talking about a piece that will last well over an hour, if not more, for three instrumental groups. The experience of writing it has been utterly extraordinary. I remember going to bed at night and wondering whether I'd be able to continue in the morning. It wasn't anything to do with having the faith to go on with it. And yet I *knew* I would be able to continue.

I went for a walk one evening, during one of those wonderful winter sunsets that you get in Greece, and I suddenly had, I suppose, what they call an out-of-body experience. I suddenly thought, I'm not a person, I'm just a piece of music. I could only see myself as music. It remains a total mystery to me. I'm looking forward to 2001 to see, or rather 'hear', what I think of it.

In *Mystagogia* – that became its title – I am using a very small orchestra split into three: this small group consists of two flutes, two oboes, two trumpets, two trombones, strings, Tibetan temple bowl, tam-tam and harp. (I have been using Tibetan temple bowls more and more in recent works because of their wonderful resonances.) The two outer orchestras are the same – one flute, one oboe, one trumpet, one trombone and strings for each. In the middle group there is harp, Tibetan temple bowl and large tam-tam. It's an intensely esoteric piece of music, and certainly not what the London Schools' Symphony Orchestra are expecting.

I think young people respond very much to concepts like this. It isn't going to be the technical difficulties, although they are quite considerable, but rather the spiritual dimension they will have to enter into that will test them. Everybody has this spiritual dimension at the core of their being and it is this they are going to have to confront, each in their own different way. It's not a question of study. One just has to tap it. For some people, it's never tapped – that's a mystery – it's like a day of sudden sunshine and calm, a well of purity suddenly discovered, a laugh of silent joy.

The Fool began almost as a result of talking to Lucy Bailey (who founded and produces the Gogmagogs) about a possible piece based on the theme of the Holy Fool. That was some time ago and I never knew whether I would do it or not. Mother Thekla's favourite kind of saint or holy man had always been the Fool. In a way she's something of a fool herself, and she wanted me to do something based on the Holy Fool; so did I. This was another form of tradition, but upside-down. Mother Thekla produced a libretto which read as if it was totally foolish; indeed completely mad.

The Byzantine Fools used to do scandalous things: they used to drop their trousers in church. They would appear to be fornicating all night over the city of Constantinople. They appeared to be total fools. On Good Friday when everybody else was fasting, they would stuff themselves with food. They denied all decency, and moral behaviour, for the sake of Christ (we could do with a few of these supreme saints in our hypocritical society today). It was an inner vocation to be a Fool, to wear funny clothes, to do all sorts of things. It's a sort of spiritual catharsis that inverts our habitual attachment to things. They were regarded as extremely holy people in Byzantine Greece and also right up to the end of the last century in Russia.

There is, however, a danger in the Fool of beginning to enjoy what you are doing (like the diabolical fool Rasputin), whereas the true Fool doesn't know what he is doing: it comes from inside. And I had to turn myself upside-down in order to compose *The Fool*, because every conceivable convention is sacrificed, all spiritual nourishment is sacrificed, all enjoyment is sacrificed. It's an exercise in total detachment from the things of this world. That is why to be a true Fool for Christ is the highest form of sanctity that can exist. As to what I was going to do with it musically, that is another matter.

The Gogmagogs are basically string players. But in *The Fool* they are going to have to sing and to act. It requires a male singer of prodigious virtuosity, not just for what he has to sing, but because of the acrobatic acting ability required. He has to turn somersaults. But in addition there has to be this inner depth of spirituality in the singer.

Symbolically he starts 'fat' and 'gross', both musically and visually; he grunts, he snores, the music itself is foolish, parodying itself, using ridiculous compositional procedures. But as the piece proceeds, a kind of agonized ecstasy comes into his vocal line. He refuses to react to any of the Orthodox Feasts that we are hearing and witnessing. The Fool loses weight as his voice radiates a hidden spiritual strength and light. At the first Feast, when he is musically gross and obscene, of course he is noticed by everyone – and revered. But at a 'Christmas party', no one sees his frail body lying on the ground. He has torn himself to shreds, broken open his own person. At Easter, amidst all the hideous secular noise, he sings an unaccompanied melody – 'He has given life'. The Fool is ignored. His voice is broken, he trembles. The world ignores him. We have shared in the image of God, but we have not bothered or given a damn to keeping it safe.

Much of my recent music is tending to put its performers to the test, and not just in technical matters, but in spiritual matters too. I sometimes worry where I am going to find such people. But one does find them, as I found Patricia Rozario for *Mary of Egypt*. Who on earth will I find for the Fool, with a virtuoso range from bottom D in the bass clef to a high falsetto G sharp in the treble clef and with the ability to interpret the unreachable heights of a Holy Fool for Christ? But there are special singers that seem to have a metaphysical understanding of music.

Maybe there always have been; people like Robert Tear, who's very much on a spiritual search, and Steven Richardson, who is not interested in music just as a career. He only does what he wants to do. If a subject interests him, then he does it. The fact that these people exist is encouraging. I required Patricia to go to an Indian spiritual master or guru in order to learn how to interpret *Agraphon*.

A piece like *Zoë* ('Life') contains passages which will require Steven Richardson to study with an Indian master. Although it's not exactly complex, it is incredibly difficult to sing, because of the abstruse rhythms which come from Samavedic rhythms. I am superimposing Samavedic rhythms not on modern music or modernistic techniques. This is my objection to Messiaen's use of Hindu rhythms – he uses Hindu rhythms as just another expressive device to serve what are basically contemporary, modernist harmonies. You can't do this. If you are taking from a tradition as deep as Hinduism you must revere the tradition as a whole, not just use bits of it as a matter of aesthetic convenience. If I use rhythmic elements from Samavedic chant, then I do so in order to create a metaphysical and musical obscurity. The words of Christ are simple, but obscure, and that is why we need the Fathers to interpret them for us. That is why I have used Samavedic rhythms for their innate sacredness and to create a 'divine obscurity'.

Zoë is about life, life everlasting. It is scored for alto flute, Tibetan temple bowl, Greek bells, bass and soprano solo and strings. Contained within it is the Gospel account of the raising of Lazarus. As I said, I use Samavedic rhythms for the music of Christ. And when I say they're difficult, they don't even add up as bars, there is no way they can add up as bars – we're talking about double-dotted semiquavers followed by minims followed by demi-semi-quavers followed by a dotted quaver. Not only are they impossible to notate, but the tempo keeps changing in every single bar. If you listen to the original primordial Samavedic chant, the only way you can notate it in a contemporary idiom is to keep changing the 'tactus' so it moves from crotchet equals, let's say, 60′ in one bar, to crotchet equals 200′ in the next bar, to crotchet equals 80′ in another bar. That is why singers trained in the Western tradition need to go to an Indian master and absorb Samavedic rhythms, before they can possibly begin to learn the part of Christ in *Zoë*.

In *Fall and Resurrection* I require a Byzantine Psaltist. Now to be a Byzantine Psaltist you have to have grown up in the tradition. It's an oral tradition which requires improvisation and which cannot possibly be taught by any Western music school. You have to go to a master. I'm not even sure then that a singer could actually 'learn' the art of singing Byzantine music. I haven't gone as far yet as writing in Byzantine notation, because to a Western singer that would mean absolutely nothing at all. So I have to 'invent' ways of being able to write this out, as I did with the Samavedic rhythms in *Zoë*. At all events performers in the future are going to have to come to grips in some way with a type of music which has not existed in Western music before.

For example, consider the problem of asking a young Indian boy singer to make the sound of an English choirboy. In a similar, if not exact, way, the average Western-trained singer cannot possibly get to the spiritual depth of a Byzantine Psaltist who has given his entire life, not to music, but primarily to God and to Christ. Maybe I'm going to have to use a Byzantine Psaltist, if I can find one. Maybe, in the future, I will be writing for traditional singers from other cultures. At the moment, however, I prefer to stay with Western singers and send them to an appropriate master.

Another example: I have written for the *nāy*, the Middle Eastern end-blown flute. I am lucky enough to have found a player in England who was actually brought up in Egypt. But this is only one person. I've written music that's not actually playable on the *nāy*, yet this player makes his own *nāys* or *kavals*, and by changing the holes he has made the playing of my music possible. The *nāy* or the *kaval* appears in both *The Toll Houses* and *Fall and Resurrection*.

*

In a series of recent eschatological works I feel that finally I have begun to find 'The Voice'. I know now that it is not a matter of finding what to say, but of how to be silent and how to hear the Spirit speaking in this silence. The Spirit alone is true; all else does not exist and Truth does not submit to any of our man-made or legalistic preparations. 'He comes to His own' – and in that moment the answer is born, the notes, the rhythm, the melody and the harmony are heard. All come into being – with no mechanical procedures, no systems, everything seems newly born and fresh, both in structure and in grace.

Blow Up the Concert Hall
and the Opera House!

BRIAN KEEBLE: *It was David Lumsdaine who led you to modernism, but your earlier music obviously had a good deal to do with modernism – its techniques and procedures, its aspirations and its relationship to the conventions of music-making in our century. But you've come to hate modernism and all it stands for. And this is not just an affectation or a passing rebellious mood, I know that there is a deeper reason for this antipathy which relates to the way in which you see modernism as a falsification of the human image. Before we go on to explore the theme of modernism, can I ask you to say what you think modernism actually is?*

JOHN TAVENER: Even before I answer that, I would like to say that we live in a time when man has not only lost his belief in God but has lost his belief in himself. And I might say that, in a certain sense, because man has lost faith in his true self he has lost his faith in God. We live in a culture in ruins, of which I believe modernism, in all its diverse manifestations, plays the leading role. My ancestor John Taverner was imprisoned by Cardinal Wolsey, but he was pardoned because he was but a musician, and I would ask the reader to pardon me because I'm not a metaphysician – I'm a musician. When I make metaphysical statements you must realize they are coming from 'but a composer'.

I would have thought that all modernists, in whatever shape or size they come, must see that we're in the grip of something terrible that is leading us, in global terms, in cosmic terms, to an unparalleled catastrophe. As to whether I think music can help to resolve this appalling dilemma, the answer is yes. *But* this music must be free of all superfluous violence. Above all, it must be free of all angst. As St Gregory of Nyssa put it, 'For it befits virtue to be free of all fear and autonomous.' The same with music. As we learn from the Liturgy, broken but not divided – separated from all but joined to all – nowhere but everywhere.

But that demands a saint in musical terms. And a saint is one who has become so simple, so transparent that he is at one with nature, and wild animals are tame in his presence. I have seen such men. Peter Brook has said Mount Athos is the only sane place left on earth. Let music follow the example of the Holy Mountain, and become a garden of the sacred – a day of sunshine and calm – a laugh or cry of silent joy/sorrow – a harp of the Spirit, breaking our hearts in cries and gestures . . . but Handel's *Semele* is doing that now, so there are no formulas.

You are implying that modernism takes account of neither the impending catastrophe nor the conditions that have caused it? Let's limit ourselves to musical modernism, although this will spill over to modernism in general. Are you saying that the modern composer must not only be aware of the imminent catastrophe, but that he has the power to change the situation?
So much modern music is taken up with the construction of musical jigsaws. I'm not saying, of course, that modern composers do not think about anything other than their music. But from my point of view, their music is an idolatry of systems, procedures and notes. If inner truth is not revealed in our music, then it is false. It is one thing to follow a spiritual inclination and another to suppose that the idolatry of 'art' is any sort of realization of the spirit.

But I'm not sure that musicians have really ever understood the meaning of the word tradition, and, as I have said before, I think it would be a marvellous thing if they could read a masterwork like René Guénon's *The Crisis of the Modern World*, where he defines very clearly and without compromise the underlying reality of this crisis.

So you are saying, quite explicitly, that music has a vital role to play in human destiny?

That must be so. If man is made in the image of God, then music for me is a process of refinding him. Modernism knows nothing about this process. How can it when it is itself a form of idolatry? It worships its notes, it worships its rhythms, it worships its techniques, it worships its colours, it worships its man-made structures – sonata form, fugue, canon, development, serialization, minimalism, the new complexity *et al* – and, perhaps worst of all, it has bound itself to a way of thinking that is barely human, let alone spiritual.

So the music of modernism, and perhaps modernism in all its forms, is actually falsifying our grasp and our understanding of what is real?
Yes, because in the case of music it worships the externalities and nothing of their inner implications – it worships just notes and procedures and nothing of the metaphysical meaning behind the notes. So far as I can hear, there is no meaning behind the notes in modernism. They are just notes for notes' sake, which is art for art's sake. If music does not assume something more than just a human response, if it does not change our life, it will leave our life outside in the terrible darkness of ignorance.

So, once man abandons or eradicates the notion that he is created in the image of God – and at least in the past the whole raison d'être of art really is tied in to the fact that man is created in the image of a higher order of reality – once man falsifies or desecrates this notion, the only things left to him are mere externalities – that is, technique, human fabrication, things 'made up' from purely human resources?
I believe that must be so. St Gregory Nazianzen said, 'Where God is not present in some form, then whatever it is does not exist at all.' I would deal with this whole problem of modernism by just saying that since it doesn't exist in the eyes of God, it doesn't truly exist. St Gregory is referring, of course, to the divine instantaneity of the Creation that all human works should, in some sense, imitate. He also said, 'All that is not

spontaneous does not exist.' And that means spontaneous in the deepest sense of the word – arising directly out of the divine presence.

This begins to underpin some of your more 'flamboyant' opinions. For instance, you've said, 'Burn down all the opera houses.' Now I begin to see what's behind what seems to be a very sweeping claim on your part.
Boulez also said burn down all the opera houses. But he had a different reason for saying so. I also say, burn down the concert halls. Stockhausen has said a similar thing. We need to find a space where, if one believes, as I do, that music is liquid metaphysics, music must inhabit a sacred *temenos* for its performance. The opera house calls to mind powdered wigs; the modern concert hall is as clinical as a hospital. We need to recover the sense of sacred space. Stockhausen wrote a piece which he instructed was to be performed 'underneath the stars', each instrument corresponding to different stars. What I think of the music is neither here nor there, but that concept is in the direction that I would like to move things. He at least responded to the archetype – perhaps that's the most important thing that the artist can do, and perhaps it is more important than the result.

You mentioned René Guénon, who has obviously influenced your thinking about the whole relationship between art and society. Have any other writers – or composers, for that matter – influenced your thinking in this respect?
Not really. At least, not in the way that Guénon influenced me. He made a very provocative remark about music: he said that after Gregorian chant the West plunged into a dark age from which we have not emerged.

All right, we've shot all the conductors, the opera houses and concert halls have all gone up in flames as well. We are still left with the problem of where music should be performed.

What underpins your idea of getting rid of a whole way of music-making is an objection to its secularism, its abstraction. Then how is music to be performed?

I'm thinking of the great medieval cathedrals of England, or of Europe. In Greece, in Epidaurus and in Ephesus, I've been very privileged to have conducted my music in these sacred spaces. So far as my own music is concerned, I dislike intensely going to concert halls. If I go to a cathedral or a sacred space it becomes a different thing, I feel a completely different person. I don't feel uncomfortable, and I don't want to dash out quickly and avoid everybody. It's no use performing a Beethoven symphony in a cathedral and there's no point in performing a piece by Harrison Birtwistle in a cathedral, because there's no connection between either.

So sacred music must have a sacred space.

Exactly. Yes.

You seem to be implying that the acoustic space of a modern concert hall is a technical abstraction, whereas the space of a cathedral has of its nature qualitative resonances of the sacred. Is this the old dichotomy of the quantitative as opposed to the qualitative?

Certainly. And I also think you could make the distinction between what is new and what is simply novel. It is totally, totally impossible for man to write anything that is new. Man can make the most ghastly noises in the world, with his voice, or by making hideous sounds on musical instruments, but he cannot make anything new. The only person who can make things new is Christ. This reminds me of the way an early disciple of Christ, Hermas, saw the Church. He saw it as having the young face of a maiden, and the white hair of wisdom and tradition. It's a question of the difference between the manipulation of externalities in a temporal context, which is the fabrication of novelty, as opposed to what Christ was referring to when He said, 'Behold I make all things new.'

From the perspective of such an ethos, then, the modern concert hall is an artificial space, even a dead space, and a cathedral is a living space?

You're absolutely right. In the clinical acoustic of modern concert halls, there is nothing for the music to resonate against. But if you perform in a medieval cathedral, my God, there is already present an eternal resonating chamber. But I insist the music must *itself* resonate against something on a higher level. We cannot open the cathedrals to modernism. Modernism in music belongs to its equivalent – modernist architecture.

Communication also comes into all this. True communication is a process whereby nourishment is taken up by living organisms, assimilated by them and turned into blood, life and strength. And it means passing on the joy of sound and metaphysics – proclaiming this miracle that defies doubt or discussion. Modernism does nothing of this. It is a mechanical collection of ever-more complex, ever-more inane formulae that are essentially dead. It cannot truly communicate. It is the antithesis of communication.

We've used the word abstraction several times. Is this the great evil of art in our time?

I think so, because it has such a limited vocabulary.

In painting it certainly has a very limited vocabulary, but it could be argued, on the other hand, that since music is in a sense 'abstract', modern music has an unparalleled musical vocabulary.

I agree on a purely musical level, modernism or abstraction in music has an unparalleled vocabulary of techniques and formulae. But at the same time it has a parallel lack of symbols, metaphysics, orientation, beauty and divinity.

However, a large musical vocabulary does not guarantee anything. Elliott Carter, for instance, works with an enormous musical vocabulary, and a formidable intelligence, but as much as I have tried I simply find that I have no reaction to his music whatsoever. The great music of the Americas comes from the Indians. And their musical vocabulary is very small in comparison with Carter. But it has a divine ray, and it is 'poor in spirit' in the deepest sense, which is far more important than being rich in vocabulary.

You're saying, then, that the considerable vocabulary of Elliott Carter none the less addresses itself to some sort of hypothetical, abstract, acoustical ear that no human being ever really possesses?

Just so, and that also explains why more and more composers go to laboratories or use computers to write their music. It seems as if science, as in almost every other sphere of our lives, is beginning to take over music. And if that is the case then music has ceased to exist.

Well, the laboratory is the inner sanctum of the scientist, where he fancies he abstracts himself from nature and stands over and above it as an objective intelligence. Can you see any connection between that and some of the manifestations of musical abstraction?

Only human beings are in the image of God and only human beings stand on the border, poised between angel and animal. This points to the human capacity to make signs – to make things which re-present realities of a higher dimension in things. We are creatures that point to our creator. The modernist has already set *himself* up as 'creator', he has wiped God out of the picture. It is just a dialogue between him and the synthesizer. God is wiped out, humanity is wiped out and so is the cosmos. Only Joe Bloggs and his computer remain. Is it even abstraction? No, it is everything goes and anything goes.

One of the presiding ideas of our time, one which permeates all levels of modern thinking, is the implicit assumption that every innovation in art need refer to nothing more than the process that is one innovation leading to the next innovation.

For some reason – I don't know quite what the reason is – our society has a fantastic thirst for innovation. We love to use the word innovation whenever we can. If you read critics, it's innovation they're looking for, the newest in this, the newest in that, the newest in everything. They fail to comprehend the metaphysical meaning of the word 'new', which is the renewal of that which always abides. The trouble is we're all too damned educated and far too damned cerebral. We must realize the limitation of the human mind, as Plato says, and go 'higher', allowing the spirit to act in us.

This evolution by innovation is nonsense to me because I don't believe in the ultimate reality of such linear development. I believe we are incarnated in the image of God in this world in order for us to re-find that heavenly celestial music from which we have been separated. Our whole life is a continuing return to the 'source'. The fact that modernism can envisage no source is a very grave and catastrophic state of affairs.

But would you agree that, because we are human and we cannot go on repeating ourselves in the same way, inevitably there has to be room for the new in art? After all, John Tavener's music is new – there is no other music like John Tavener's music. So how does this element of newness arise? In what can its newness consist?

Instead of thinking of it as a manipulation of externalities in a temporal context, one has to think of a rekindling of the ethos of the eternal. Now what precisely do I mean by that? Of course, in some ways it is very difficult to answer because the language of rational dialectic cannot encompass such things. In certain pieces I don't know where the music comes from. But there are certain things that one can do.

I think it's an appalling state of affairs that many young composers are persuaded to regard such works as Schoenberg's *Erwartung*, *Pierrot Lunaire*, Berg's *Lulu*, Boulez's *Le Marteau sans Maître* and Stockhausen's *Gruppen* as examples of music to be revered. Starting from such examples of over-sophisticated contrivance, where on earth could they go? Wouldn't their time be better spent in contemplating the primordial origins of music? The great Taoists, ancient Chinese philosophers, said that music appeared at the beginning of all things. Well, if that is the case, then we have to investigate what this means. If it really did occur at the beginning of all things then we should at least attempt to find out how we can get back to this primordial state of music. There are non-man-made Byzantine magic squares, music of the spheres, sacred tone systems of various countries, and of course all sacred tone systems connect one to another.

Byzantine chant, for instance, comes to us from Pythagoras through the ancient Hellenic world, mixed with the music of the Synagogue sung during Christ's lifetime. So, like the ikon, the chant has an Apostolic succession. All this has been totally forgotten or just ignored by the modern world. The great scholar of Sufi metaphysics, Henry Corbin, referred to the Other World, the world of the imagination of the soul, as the *imaginal* world. 'The pilgrim, rising from one degree to another, discovers on each higher level a subtle state, a more entrancing beauty, a more intense spirituality, a more flowing delight.' It was in the celestial world that Pythagoras heard the music of the spheres. As a result of what he had heard, he perfected the science of music. All this forgotten knowledge – and there are volumes written on it – only highlights the appalling poverty of modernism. But to rediscover these sacred forms one has to forget time altogether because such knowledge somehow resists being accommodated to the flow of history.

Some of the most wonderful music ever written was written in Russia at the time of Ivan the Terrible. The Orthodox services were vastly long because the Word had to be completely clear. So Ivan the Terrible sent off all his musical experts to neighbouring Poland and they sneaked into the back of Roman Catholic cathedrals and heard this (to their ears) astonishing counterpoint of the West, which, of course, got through the text more quickly. What was so marvellous was the fact that they came back knowing nothing of the rules of Western counterpoint, and they wrote this utterly stunning music – full of dissonance, full of vision: you could not place it in time, although at times it sounds like late Stravinsky. With the help of Father Michael Fortounatto and Peter Phillips we put together a disc of this music, which was 'realized'. It is stunningly dissonant, not cleverly dissonant in the way that Purcell or Gesualdo are. I defy any one to analyse this music.

The Taoist philosopher you mentioned, when he talked about a beginning, of course had in mind an eternal beginning, not a temporal beginning. And this brings us to one of the great bugbears of the West, that is, its obsession with sacrificing everything on the altar of historical determinism. The West must relearn how to situate consciousness above the level of temporal succession. Surely the whole question of development in musical forms is related to this type of mentality that seeks to elaborate the means of a forward progression?
I think we have to go back. I think in the end intuition teaches us everything. Leave the universities of the world and go into the universities of the desert. So say the Fathers. I am, of course, talking about metaphysical intuition; the only way still unexplored by our modernist hell.

First of all, one has to say we know nothing, and from that abyss we must abandon all preconceived ideas, whether it be serialism, sonata form, development, fugue, canon and so on, and get rid of it all, so that one has nothing left in one's mind to begin with. It feels like an abyss. This does, of course, presuppose that one believes in some kind of higher reality. But even if not, let the young composer try to forget everything he or she knows, just to see what happens. If it's just silence, then okay, it's just silence. If it's just one or two banal notes, okay, then it's just one or two banal notes. But I guarantee that if one continues with this, gradually a music starts to form inside one, and who knows, we might start to realize that another kind of reality does after all exist.

You're saying then that the composer has to work on himself . . .
Absolutely.

. . . as much as on his music?
Almost more so, I think. Let the abyss be filled with oceans of
light. Or with nothing. In a way this is the 'litmus test', both for
modernists and for traditionalists.

*To discover some affinity with the inner harmonies in his own
being.*
Yes, yes.

*In what way is the more recent simplicity of your musical lan-
guage the result of your having purged yourself deliberately of
much of the means of Western music-making?*
I have rejected much of the intellectualism of Western music
with its formal, self-imposed constrictions which inhibit and
enchain me. Of course, Byzantine music has 'constrictions' but
these liberate me by turning me inside out, as it were. It has made
me tear myself to shreds and left me hanging on by a thread of
simplicity and, I hope, serenity. At least that is how it seems to
me.

We have to become 'foolish', as the Holy Fools of old, then we
can begin to grasp that a man who thinks he is somebody important is symbolically in fact 'fat and grotesque'. Only when he has
realized that he is *nothing* can his soul grow. At this point the
purging begins. But this is not a characteristic of Western music
as a whole. I have tried to symbolize something of all of this in
The Fool, both musically and dramatically.

*What would you say to people who might suggest that you are
being very unfair about modern music? After all, your music,
although it's very different (in more recent years) from modern
music in both its intention and its realization, none the less it
makes use of the apparatus of contemporary music-making.
Have you nothing good to say about modernism at all?*

I have definitely positive things to say about modern music. I have positive things to say about Webern, and about late Stravinsky. I have some positive things to say about Messiaen and about Stockhausen. Because I feel in the works of these composers there is a cosmic dimension.

Your music has been labelled, along with that of Arvo Pärt, as being 'holy minimalism'. How do you react to that?
It's a facetious journalistic caption. As far as minimalism is concerned (let's leave out the 'holy' for the moment), minimalism means absolutely nothing at all to me. In fact, I'd almost prefer the 'new complexity', because I find minimalism is just purely computer music for idiots. As far as 'holy minimalism' is concerned, I don't think these journalists quite know what they're saying, because holy minimalism in Orthodox tradition refers to the very early writings on prayer called the Apophthegmata. This was written in about the second and third centuries in Egypt, and it talks about the importance of using very few words in prayer, like 'help me', 'save me', 'come and do your will in me'. We hardly know what we need.

These masters are wrapped in a depth of inner silence of which we have no idea today, and taught by *being*, not by speech. 'If a man cannot understand my silence, he will never understand my words.'

You haven't actually said anything about beauty – we might come to that on another occasion. Do you associate modernism with ugliness, as being somehow inextricably associated with it?
Well, it's got nothing to do with ugly sounds on their own. That is naïve in the extreme. Dostoevsky said that the world could only be saved by beauty. But I think he was referring to a beauty beyond this world; ultimately the Beauty of God. Otherwise, it is sentimental.

Cecil Collins suggested that modernism lacked the context of redemption. I certainly find this is so with the paintings of Francis Bacon and the works of his musical 'brother' Harrison

Birtwistle. But I am not just dismissing these artists because they do not believe in redemption or divine realities. As Dostoevsky said, 'Either God, or everything goes.' I strongly dislike the aggressive masculinity in much modernism. I think naked putrefaction can exist provided there is a metaphysical point to it. For everything presupposes its opposite. On its own, for its own sake, it is nothing. It's literally 'rot'. If one relates putrefaction to the much weaker word 'ugliness', one can say that putrefaction is the journey through the Inferno where one must behold man's every sin, without which the work cannot proceed with its purgative process and paradisal conclusion. But I do not credit modernism with doing anything of this kind.

After the castigation that you've given modernism, it's a little surprising that you should have enthusiasm for a composer like Webern, who many people will see as one of the greatest composers of modern music.
There's a whole cluster of composers that came after Webern: they take his fragmentation, they take the shell, the exterior, they take everything that's exoteric in Webern, and seem to me not to comprehend what lies beyond the notes, or in his case one might say what is 'inside' the notes. For me, Webern is really not a modernist at all; he's one of the few composers who understood the concept of silent music, which is a very mystical concept.

Can I suggest a 'nature mystic', because he saw music as an extension of nature?
He saw music as an extension of nature, yes, but then, what is nature? It's God in nature. He was a very devout Roman Catholic. And he seems to have been able to 'transubstantiate' the human fabrication of Schoenberg's system. I think it was David Jones who used to say that a work of art was never finished until it has become 'transubstantiated'. I think Webern actually would have agreed with him on this. And the inner silence, metaphysical silence, of Webern is almost unique in our time.

I'd like to suggest that it's not 'metaphysical silence' but an abstract yet qualitative silence, a silence that restores the cognitive weight of tones.

What do you mean by that?

That he restores, for the first time in centuries of Western music, the sense of there being something 'beyond', yet at the heart of sound; the sense that the notes refer to another order of reality. We hear this in organum, for instance. But it's an aspect of sound that has gradually been lost to Western music. His silence is not just absence of sound, as in most composers. With Webern the silence is an integral part of what we actually hear.

For me, the silence of the last movement of the *Piano Variations* is almost unbearable; it's very complex music and yet it sounds so simple – it's really monody, it's a kind of fragmented monody. But it's so beautiful, and the composers who imitate that fragmented monody have nothing. No one can explain this metaphysical depth that Webern had – he just had it.

How ascetic and unique is this music. His last work *Das Augenlicht*, with its metaphysical subtext relating to the Mass, is miraculous, especially the final canon. But in a way Webern is too scholastic, too dry for my ear. He reminds me rather of Thomas Aquinas looking for the exact number of angels dancing on the head of a pin. Webern found his twelve notes on plants – I love him for that, and for his conducting his own arrangement of Schubert dances.

*

We have spoken about Webern. There are three other modern composers that I would like to single out for special comment.

There's late Stravinsky. If ever I've had a conducting ambition, it has been to conduct *Threni, Canticum Sacrum* and *Abraham and Isaac* in a building like Salisbury Cathedral, because I've never heard satisfactory performances of any of these masterworks. Stravinsky transfigures Schoenberg's system almost into the sacred. He goes as far as any Western man can in providing a kind of non-traditional archaic sacredness, and of course this comes about through his Orthodoxy, and never forgetting his astonishing ear. I love the *Canticum*, with its solemn, sobre dedication to the apostle Mark, then the command of Christ to go into the world and preach the gospel, and then that exquisite tenor solo, 'Surge Aquilo', with its Byzantine flavour. Then the extraordinary setting of the Latin words '*Credidi*' and the final section which is a perfect palindrome of the first section.

I love *Threni* for its almost cosmic groans at the beginning from the orchestra, and then the heart-rending '*Plorans ploravit in nocte*'.

Abraham and Isaac, the strangely archaic setting of Hebrew – archaic, and yet serial. Stravinsky was basically a modernist but, as I have said, his salvation was his Orthodoxy and, of course, his ear. I regard the *Canticum sacrum*, *Threni* and *Abraham and Isaac* as the three masterworks of this century.

Oliver Messiaen. I love his early music – works like the *Quartet for the End of Time* and *Vingt regards*: there is a spontaneity about this music and it is much more esoteric than the later music. I should say that he is one of the most important composers of this century, but he is a one-off (not unlike Blake in that sense), with his deeply personal and therefore non-traditional brand of mysticism, with which I personally have little in common. But his name is written in the heavens and he cannot be dismissed. He could not resist modernism; indeed, he taught it to his pupils. There are traditional elements in his music, like Hindu rhythms, but, as I have said earlier, one cannot take something as sacred and esoteric as Hindu rhythms as just another coloration for one's aesthetic palette and place them over modernist harmonies.

Chronochromie makes me want to scream; *Et Expecto Resurrectionem Mortuorum* impressed me deeply at its first performance. But I heard it again the other day by accident on Greek radio and I found it far too exoteric, far too gestural, far too noisy, and perhaps a little bit empty. But I am temperamentally out of tune with Messiaen, and perhaps in the long run I am the loser.

Last of all, Stockhausen. Stockhausen has burst the bounds of conventional modern music-making with something of a cosmic vision. He cannot possibly be dismissed. A perfect work, like *Stimmung*, is pure tradition. The chord that he uses is from the harmony of the spheres, and the manner of singing it again is pure tradition.

But the megalomania in Stockhausen cannot stop him from inserting his own inane erotic poems into *Stimmung*, such as 'Pee, pee, pee on my little tree; ah, that is warm'. Stockhausen had wonderful ideas which often border on traditional ideas but to my ears the musical result has a kind of seediness about it, and more often than not I can't help feeling that the music is best left unheard – because as yet Stockhausen seems unable to transcend mere human contrivance. But his name, like Messiaen's, has been written in the heavens. I love the idea of him working with his family – it is a wonderful traditional idea – and I find the concept of his operas for every day of the week quite marvellous, and they certainly have their moments, their amazing moments. Perhaps Stockhausen could be the Scriabin of the twentieth century or, at his most cosmic, without any of his inanity, he could be the musical equivalent in breadth and stature of St.-John Perse, one of the greatest poets of our time.

A Land of Poets and Ikons

This lower world is an exile while being at the same time a reflection of Paradise.

Frithjof Schuon

BRIAN KEEBLE: *I have heard you say on more than one occasion that you feel more at home in Greece than you do in England. What exactly do you mean by 'at home'?*

JOHN TAVENER: I actually feel physically better. I write much quicker in Greece than I do in England and, perhaps most important of all, when I look at the landscape, I find because it's so ancient it helps me to know if I've got things right in the music that I'm writing. I love the landscape and I have a deep nostalgia for Greece. I have no nostalgia for England, although I'm very happy that I live in England as well as going to Greece. I think I feel at home in Greece because it's a country that contains everything I hold dear. 'Everywhere I travel, Greece wounds me, she wounds me with her beauty – perfumes of silence and pine.'

Has this obviously purely intuitive process got something to do with the physical fact that you are in an environment that suits you and you can then tell if anything jars, or is out of order?
It's very difficult to explain, because it's a mystery to me. If I look at the Sussex Downs from my home in England I don't have that reaction, but curiously I do in Greece. There's no other country in the world where I've felt this – only Greece. 'There you see, I love those poplars . . . raising their shoulders into the sun.'

What about the culture of Greece?
Well, if one's talking about Byzantine or ancient culture it's vast,

but in the culture of Greece in the twentieth century as far as I can see, musically not very much has happened.

The mythology of the ancient world and the glory of Orthodoxy seem to crown the Acropolis. It's as if all the threads of Greek tradition are woven together into a glorious eternal present – all the way down from Homer to the present day, like Byzantine music, stemming from ancient Greece. There has never been a renaissance in Greece, there's never been a reformation, so it is perfectly natural that the tradition flows in one long unbroken line, and this is very attractive to me.

There have been contemporary poets of great significance in the twentieth century, and they all possess the richly traditional voice of previous ages. I was introduced to them by Philip Sherrard and Petros Morisinis. Sometimes I set them in Greek and sometimes I set them in English, depending on the translation and what exactly I want. Poets like Kalvos, Seferis, Sikelianos, Cavafy, Solomos. Take someone like Seferis, who would be something of the order of Eliot in terms of distinction. The marvellous thing about Seferis is that his poetry is known to the average man on the streets. Greece must be one of the few countries in the world where poetry can be quoted in this way. I remember quoting to a Greek the opening of my *Sixteen Haiku of Seferis*:

Στάξε στὴ λίμνη   Spill into the lake
  μόνο μιὰ στάλα κρασί   but a drop of wine

and he could actually continue:

  καὶ σβήνει ὁ ἥλιος   and the sun vanishes

You can't imagine in England quoting a bit of T. S. Eliot's *Four Quartets* and the same thing happening. And this was just an ordinary man. But you could also do this with the Greek Patristic Fathers and the same thing will happen. What a way to communicate!

Perhaps a lot of the reason for this is because the Greek popular composers – people like Theodorakis, Hajadaikis – set this great poetry to music: and the people love the music, so they love the poetry.

You couldn't have those popular composers in a place like Eng-land, where the sense of tradition is almost non-existent.
Non-existent I would say, yes.

It obviously must have something to do with their Orthodox faith? From what I know of Greece, Orthodoxy itself is more suffused throughout all levels of society. In England, religion is kept for Sunday; here (in Greece), it's every day and all day.
It's every day. And you see Greek people, before they go in to swim, they cross themselves. I've been on many hair-raising journeys with young taxi drivers and every time they pass a little *ikonostasis* on the side of the road they cross themselves three times. One often finds shrines going up a mountain pass where somebody probably met their death in some accident. Every time they pass a church they make the sign of the cross three times. It's something deeply engraved into the Greek psyche. It's a country rich in metaphysics, for goodness sake, it's a country of tradi-tion. It doesn't surprise me in the least that Orthodoxy crowned the Parthenon.

Also, the chant of Greece is a kind of collection of the concepts of Plato about intervals, about the sacred science of music in the mathematics of Pythagoras, and music from an even more ancient Greece. So Christianity was, in a way, like a continua-tion and fulfilment, as it is from the Old Testament. The Greeks proceed in an almost unbroken line from Plato to Byzantium. It is an amalgam of all things Greek, past and present. Greek Orthodoxy, as I said earlier, has an apostolic succession in music, because it contains the music sung in the synagogues dur-ing the lifetime of Christ, the mathematics from Pythagoras, and the ethos of Plato. So one could say, rather like ikons, Byzantine music is the prototype and there is no greater Christian music.

And this sense of the primordial that many Greeks still possess is underscored by the landscape, which itself seems to be an expression of the eternal.

> Among the bones music: it crosses the sand,
> Crosses the sea. Among the bones a flute's sound,
> The distant sound of a drum, and the faint ringing
> Of bells crosses the dry fields, crosses the dolphined sea.

It resonates from the eternal.

Whereas in England, of course, the landscape is man-made and changing, but here it's a very static landscape.
I very often feel, especially in certain places I go to, that this landscape was here, just as it is now, when Homer was alive or when Plato or Aristotle was still alive.

Would all these thoughts be connected with something I've heard you say several times, which is that you wouldn't have to say a lot about metaphysics to a Greek: he would understand in an intuitive sort of way, whereas to an Englishman metaphysics is a very abstruse and remote subject about which he probably knows nothing?
To Greeks you wouldn't have to explain about the 'intellective organ of the heart' – every time they venerate an ikon, after all, they do so with the 'intellective organ of the heart'. It's not a question of human emotions, it's got nothing to do with the human intelligence; it's venerated with that intellective organ of the heart. And the same applies to the veneration of the relics of saints.

Why do you think the poetry of Greece isn't appreciated outside Greece as much as it should be?
I think you have to love Greece very much to understand its imagery; it's full of images of the sea, images of ancient Greece, images of Byzantine Greece. It is very much a Greek affair in that way. To fully understand Cavafy, for instance, one must know something of the Greco-Alexandrian world. 'Listen – your final

pleasure – to the voices, to the exquisite music of that strange procession, and say goodbye to her, to the Alexandria you are losing.'

You must come to Greece first?
Maybe you must, yes. I've been coming here for the last thirty years, so it's not surprising that I can quote Greek poetry from Sappho to Sikelianos without often knowing which is which, so strong is the tradition.

> . . . those memorials of the exile of the sons of Clearax;
> for these . . . wasted dreadfully away . . .

It is surely some of the greatest poetry that has ever been written. I think the people I mentioned – Kalvos, Solomos, Sikelianos, Cavafy and Seferis – have a sense of tradition, unlike Eliot, whom I regard as a modernist, and who at his best can write about this traditional state but actually is never able to express it poetically as a theophony, as it were. The Greek poets in general feel to me to be much closer to Yeats, who I think is the greatest Western poet of the twentieth century, especially in the late poetry, because he is also timeless and traditional, like the Greeks.

Part of Yeats's sense of tradition was Greek, of course. The Byzantine culture meant a great deal to him, also Homer and the Greek dramatists. You mentioned that you always set your Greek poets in English, but you've done the Haiku of Seferis in Greek.
I don't always set them in English. With Kalvos, for instance, in his monumental poem *Eis Thanaton* – 'To Death' – that was set in Greek. But the two Cavafy settings I set in English. And I have finished a massive *Tribute to Cavafy* which will be in both English and Greek, for chorus, speaker, bells and Tibetan temple bowl.

How did you decide, English or Greek?
It depends on the quality of the translation. With *Sixteen Haiku*

of Seferis, I took one look at the first verse, the verse quoted to the 'ordinary Greek' I referred to – 'Στάξε στὴ λίμνη . . .'. If you put that into English, although it's very well translated by Philip Sherrard, it doesn't resonate with a rhythm: 'Spill into the lake but a drop of wine and the sun vanishes' – that just doesn't work. But then you take a poem like 'Agraphon': it's magnificent English in Philip's translation – 'And now Lord I, the very least of men . . . stand before you . . . grant me, Lord . . . one single moment of Your Holy calm' and so on. The English captures so well the 'tragic weight' of the original Greek.

Are the Greek poets, with their deeper sense of tradition, any sort of standard for you when you turn to setting English poetry?
No. When I set Yeats or Blake or Eliot or Donne or George Herbert, I have a completely different approach. Maybe the only one that has a similarity is Yeats. I can see a similarity between Yeats and the twentieth-century poets of Greece – there is something in common between Ireland and Greece. I love both countries. I love Greece more, but when I go to Bantry Bay in West Cork, as I often do, to the festival there, it's one of the most magical landscapes in the world. But my affection for it is not as deep as it is for Greece.

This takes us back to the Celtic saints. The Celtic saints were much more like the great saints of the early Orthodox faith. Indeed, the Celtic saints are great saints of the Orthodox Church because they appeared before the Schism. There is the same identification with nature, the same outdoor life. In Greece or in Egypt it would have been in the desert, whereas the Celtic saints lived on little rocky islands in conditions of great, great austerity. I would say they were not scholastics in any kind of way. The Divine Truth was revealed to them, in their lives of poverty and in their love of God's earth. Thank God there was none of the overrated social consciousness ethics and morality (the precursor of humanism) in their spirituality.

You used Irish keening in the Celtic Requiem.
Keening is something Ireland and Greece have in common; at funerals in both countries, especially at the graveside in Greece, the mourners express themselves in a spine-chilling howling. This is a very good thing because it releases the grief in a perfectly natural and, as I say, primordial way.

Talking about Greece inevitably brings us to the subject of ikons. You are inextricably connected with ikons: people think of ikons now when they think of your music. With Mary of Egypt *you were at great pains to explain that this was not an opera but a 'moving ikon'. Appreciation of ikons does not come too readily to an Anglo-Saxon. How did you come to your understanding of them?*
I was in an art gallery somewhere, as I have said elsewhere – this was long before I was an Orthodox, at about the age of nineteen – and there was a tiny painting in the corner which, I discovered, was an ikon. That was my introduction to the ikon. All the other paintings round it seemed to fade into nothing in comparison. To me, it is the most transcendent form of art that exists in the West – that is, if you can call it art in the conventional sense. Whether you can write music that is truly like an ikon, whether you can prostrate in front of a piece of music, I simply do not know. I suppose the closest you get to it is in the chant that goes with the ikonography of the Church. I might also say that an ikon dissects us, and I think truly sacred music should do the same.

By that, I mean that the ikon is there in front of you and you can see it, comforting and clear, day and night. Whether your eyes are open or shut, you do not lose the presence of the uncreated light. Whether you live or die, it keeps you cradled in life incorruptible. It is a new star leading to the King of peace. It is a life-giving presence. It dissects you by bringing you into an area where everything is true, free from sorrow. You fall down before it and kiss it. You receive life from it. The average Western art critic is at a loss when confronted by an ikon, it disarms him because he cannot dissect it in that cerebral way he is trained to do. He must simply empty himself before it, or walk away; which is what he almost always does.

The ikon has a far more direct link with the Divine Presence, which itself precludes the criteria of what we conventionally think of as art criticism. One simply cannot approach an ikon in this way.

I could go to the extreme and say that in order to appreciate or comprehend an ikon fully, you must first be baptized in the Orthodox Church in the name of the Father, the Son and the Holy Spirit. This is certainly the view that many Athonite monks hold. You actually 'read' an ikon, that's the right word – you don't look at it, you 'read' it. And you 'write' it rather than paint it.

The first thing you do when you enter an Orthodox church is venerate an ikon. When you go in a Roman Catholic church the first thing you do is genuflect in front of the reserved sacrament. Of course there is a sacrament reserved on the altar for the sick, in the Orthodox church, but it isn't the first thing we venerate; it is the ikon. The ikon is the meeting of the created and the uncreated. It is above all a witness to the Incarnation.

I'm willing to accept that those Renaissance paintings to which I referred earlier, especially the late ones of plump Italian women holding well-fed Florentine babies, are very well executed and they may well be more 'beautiful' than an ikon in a sensuous way. But such paintings have nothing to do with the sacred; nothing to do with true beauty. By contrast the ikon embodies the divine prototype; the Mother of God is painted holding her child. It doesn't look like a child we might know, it is already 'theology'. The Mother of God points to her child, who is represented as *puer senex*; His hair is balding, His face is old and full of wisdom. The Orthodox would never paint Christ, even as a child, in a sentimental way. He is already the saviour of mankind. The way of the Italian Renaissance and all Western religious art, right up to the present day, is a removal of the sacred in favour of the human ego.

1. JT's mother (*c.* 1940).

2. JT with his father in Greece (1992).

3. JT aged 4 (1948).   4. JT aged 18 (1962)

5. Stravinsky and Rostropovich at the Royal Academy of Music (*c.* 1968).
JT and his brother in the background.

6. Mother Thekla (1946).
7. JT with Mother Thekla at the Monastery of the Assumption (1989)

8. JT with his wife Maryanna and daughters Sofia and Theodora (1999).

9. JT with Steven Isserlis in the Greek Orthodox Cathedral in London (1994).
10. Patricia Rozario as Mary of Egypt (1992).

Byzantine Palindrome

from a fountain in Constantinople

Ν Ι Ψ Ο Ν   ΑΝΟΜΗΜΑΤΑ   ΜΗ   ΜΟΝΑΝ   ΟΨΙΝ

Cleanse   the sins   not   only   the face

11. Byzantine Palindrome from a fountain in Constantinople.

Challispress Limited 34 Hollingworth Court, Ashford Road, Maidstone, Kent 0622-683886

ms 20st

12. A page from the score of *Fall and Resurrection*.

13. The Taveners' house in Greece. 14. JT conducting a rehearsal of
The Apocalypse at the amphitheatre in Ephesus (1995).

15. Philip Sherrard (*c.* 1996).
16. *Ikon of The Resurrection* by Kiril Sokolov.

17. JT with Petros Morosinis, Andreas and JT's elder daughter, Theodora, in a kafeneion in Aigina, Greece (1995). 18. Frithjof Schuon (1991).

19. Cecil Collins (*c.* 1965).

20. JT with Brian Keeble in Greece, while working on *The Music of Silence* (1998).

21. JT greeting HRH The Prince of Wales on his 50th birthday (1998).

The more you depict holy figures, saints and Christ even, in a realistic fashion, the more the viewer has to presuppose that the painter actually saw these people, which is itself produces an absurdity.

Absolutely. Whereas, according to tradition, we have a prototype in the ikon in so far as St Luke painted the Mother of God. And the prototype for the head of Christ, Orthodox tradition believes, is that when Christ was unable to visit the King of Edessa He miraculously imprinted an image of His face on to a cloth. He sent to King Abgar this ikon 'made without hands', and it's from these prototypes that the first ikons were derived.

There's a spiritual affinity, too, between ikons and chant, because chant, in the same way as do ikons, resists the sort of critical assessment to which the modern mind has become so habituated.

Chant, no less than the ikon, dissects us, or makes no impression on us whatsoever. Of course, living in the kind of mad world that we do, I'm sure that there are a lot of people to whom chant means nothing whatever.

It takes quite an effort to approach chant and ikons. At least in so far as you have to put aside as inappropriate an accumulated apparatus of preconceived ideas about the nature and purpose of art.

Both chant and ikons reduce this worldly sophistication to a nullity. In that sense they're both totally dead to the world. They have nothing to do with the world, they have gone outside the world. There may be more 'clever' music, there may be more 'clever' paintings, more 'attractive' and 'pleasing' paintings. But such qualities belong to a kind of art that does not reach the high level on which ikons and chant exist. In a certain sense you have to be something of a saint to be able to paint an ikon and write chant. There are a lot of very bad ikons being painted in the twentieth century. I say bad because they are departing from the prototype. In these you see hideous departures from the norm, like those dreadful Roman Catholic pictures of Christ with long blond hair looking like a film star.

Can I suggest that they're not bad, but that they are incorrect?
But then we have a paradox. Sometimes these 'incorrect' ikons, as you put it, are the miracle-working ones and not those we think of as the great ikons of the Byzantine period, or ikons by Andrei Rublev. That greatly pleased Metropolitan Anthony. Philip Sherrard said, rather typically, that the quality of the miracles must have been bloody awful.

Now, let me make a thoroughly scurrilous accusation. Couldn't it be said that in your music you are putting long blond hair on the tones of Byzantine chant?
Yes! Well, I'm not Greek, I'm not Russian, I'm not Egyptian. What am I to do? It's not for me to answer the question. But it is a very serious question and yes, Brian, a thoroughly scurrilous suggestion!

It's a question that's related to something we have mentioned before; that it is inescapable that an artist in the twentieth century will find it simply impossible to escape every measure of individualism – it's unavoidable. And of course it's also related to the response you got when you set the Liturgy. You were accused of 'making it all up'. That's the equivalent of saying, 'But you've put long blond hair on Christ', is it not?
It's certainly paradoxical. But I wouldn't do that now. If I was asked to set the Liturgy I would have to think very hard about it now. If England was ever to become an Orthodox country it would have to have its own sacred tone system. That would take hundreds of years. But an interesting parallel to 'putting blond hair on ikons' is the way that pagan Russia, in the ninth century, decided that it wanted to become Christian. The ruler sent out envoys, both to Rome and to Constantinople, and when they arrived in Constantinople they were so overwhelmed by the beauty of the Liturgy they said, 'We didn't know whether we

were in heaven or whether we were on earth.' So they became Orthodox and brought all the Greek neumes back and they started singing them.

To begin with, they sang exactly what was written. Over hundreds of years they kept these books in front of them but the chant started to change. If you look at the Znamenny chant, or the early medieval chants of Russia now, you cannot see any connection between the sacred Byzantine tones and the sacred tones of Russia.

So, to come back to your scurrilous suggestion, in a sort of way I try to do the same thing. I look at the chant in a different way though, because I'm not going to live for hundreds of years, and somewhere in the recreative process it undergoes a metamorphosis and becomes something totally different. As a composer I would argue with an absolutist traditionalist who would no doubt say that I had abandoned the Apostolic tradition. I would simply have to say, 'The Spirit listeth where it will'. That does not mean I believe in or would advocate a general 'free for all'; it rather means a mysterious *continuation*: not development, but a recreation.

I understand what you've said and I can see from the point of view of being a composer what your dilemma is in approaching a hieratic art like chant. Your use of chant lifts your music to a level beyond mere self-expression, yet what you write must be, in some sense, part of your personal experience – or else it would be false. Is what you're attempting in your music in relation to chant and ikons related to the idea that the hieratic prototype is in some sense no longer valid in its older forms?
I see what you are asking, but I'm not sure quite how to answer. Certainly people do go on painting ikons by copying earlier examples. I remember the Patriarch of Alexandria came over to England and one of the first things he did was to be shown an exhibition of recently painted ikons. I happened to be with him when he was looking at them, and he said, 'Yes, these are very good reproductions of Byzantine ikons. But where's the spirit?' And that's the danger.

Take the work of the Renaissance painter and that of the Byzantine ikonographer. The one is the creation of someone's artistic talent, the other the reflection and flower of liturgical life. The one is of *this* world and that's where it leaves you. The other rises up from the deepest level at which everything in man is united. Whether this unity is 'actualized' as a result of our experience of chant and ikons is another matter. But I believe that on somewhere like Mount Athos (and not only there), this state of inner unity is still realizable – the same, yesterday, today and forever. The notion that chant has died, or the ikon has died, is tantamount to saying 'Christ is dead forever.'

In Greece, there is a huge revival of monasticism. Young lawyers, doctors and scientists are leaving their jobs to go and become monks on the Holy Mountain. As long as one single person in the world can produce great chant, as long as one single person can paint an authentic ikon, then the world will continue to exist. And with this huge revival on the Holy Mountain, it seems that the world *will* continue to exist. And this is where I personally have to withdraw from the picture.

As I have already said, we are living in a culture in ruins. The times are not propitious and there are no absolutes in the creative arts. I have never attempted to write chant, but rather to find what that ethos of compunction, of humility, of certitude is, and also the prelapsarian innocence which chant at its best has. I attempt to take that ethos and try somehow, from the silence of ikons and the silence of chant, to reinstate both qualities into my music.

Liquid Metaphysics

The sacred is the interference of the uncreated in the created, of the eternal in time, of the infinite in space, of the
supraformal in forms; it is the mysterious introduction
into one realm of existence of a presence which in reality
contains and transcends that realm and could cause it to
burst asunder in a sort of divine explosion. The sacred is
the incommensurable, the transcendent, hidden within a
fragile form belonging to this world; it has its own precise
rules, its terrible aspects and its merciful action; moreover,
any violation of the sacred, even in art, has incalculable
repercussions. Intrinsically the sacred is inviolable, and so
much so that any attempted violation recoils on the head
of the violator.

Frithjof Schuon

BRIAN KEEBLE: *You have referred to your music as 'liquid metaphysics' and you have frequently used the words 'metaphysics'
and 'tradition'. Perhaps we should now investigate these ideas,
to see how you understand them, both in a musical and in a non-
musical sense, since both concepts have a bearing beyond music.
What do you understand by the word 'metaphysics'?*

JOHN TAVENER: I regard metaphysics as a fountainhead through
which all music must flow, and I think the key word is 'flow'. As
St Irenaeus of Lyons said, 'God will always have something more
to teach man, and man will always have something more to learn
from God.' I return to the key word, flow. It's not a cerebral
process – it's a question of having the humility to leave oneself
vulnerable and allow the Spirit to flow through one. If you go
back to the great masters, the saints and certain poets like St
Simeon the New Theologian, he always received his poetry as
pure vision.

I suppose if you take the greatest example of all in this respect it would be St John the Theologian, who wrote the Apocalypse. That was one colossal vision, and he saw 'everything'. St Ephrem the Syrian, the poet, also had his poetry revealed to him. Then there are all the Desert Fathers, whether they be the early Egyptian Fathers that I've mentioned (in the Apophthegmata), or people like St Dionysios the Areopagite and St Gregory Nazienzen. It's clearly a revealed tradition, it all comes from the 'university of the desert'. It is a question of being still and listening to the voice inside one.

You've always written music out of the belief that it can communicate with a level of reality beyond this world – even more powerfully during the last twenty years. And anyone who has even a slight knowledge of your music can see that your concern with metaphysics does not come entirely from the musical world itself. What have been the main non-musical sources for this concern in relation to the specific problems of being a composer during the second half of the twentieth century?
I've read many works by people who have written about tradition, like René Guénon, Philip Sherrard, A. K. Coomaraswamy, Frithjof Schuon, etc. One can study Machaut, Bach, Stravinsky and Messiaen but this is not enough. If one truly wants to rediscover the sacred in music, one must go outside music and return to the Gospels, the Fathers and the sayings of the Sufis too, in order to understand this non-scholastic, non-developmental approach to music. In the end, the glory of music is inseparable from the superabundance of life.

Closely allied to metaphysics, of course, is the notion of tradition. Do you see a distinction between metaphysics and tradition?
Not really. I think both lead us to God, unless you're just playing onanistic intellectual games with tradition.

So you would make a firm distinction between tradition in the

esoteric sense and the common notion of tradition as simply being historical precedent, which doesn't interest you at all?
Not at all. Changing guards at Buckingham Palace.

We are, then, talking about a supra-human level of reality and what it takes to be in contact with it? Now this must entail a level of reality that itself calls into question the meanings and values we attach to the events that make up history. Is this the basis on which you have come to consider the inherent limitations of modernism, with its emphasis on development?
To answer that question as simply as I possibly can, I need to go back to 1977. When I joined the Orthodox Church and Metropolitan Anthony asked me to set to music the Liturgy of St John Chrysostom, I did it in the only way I knew how. I suppose you could say what I wrote then was very much a Western-orientated sacred music, but it is not what I understand by sacred music any more. I just wrote as sparely as I possibly could, using just a small collection of notes.

I don't think I can stress strongly enough the difference between the Latin West and the Greek East. The Latin West has condemned itself and bound itself to what is human – 'the mind that is set on the flesh is hostile to God; it does not submit to God's Law, indeed it cannot'. Even as far back as the eleventh century, a Greek observer was concerned with the goings-on in Notre Dame in Paris: 'Now they are imposing their own wills on chant, writing frivolous descants over it, and "organum" to accompany it.' This was and still is to some extent anathema to the Orthodox. 'We are not contending against flesh and blood.'

Doubtless it's a sweeping generalization, but the Latin West tends to look to the world, whereas the Greek East tends to look to what is beyond the world. I suppose I have been privileged to suffer from a life-threatening illness. Every day of my life could be my last, which means that death is always in front of my eyes. Death is a spouse, so to speak. Therefore, I can often not distinguish between this world and the world to come. But I am no saint and not a monk but I can say with all sobriety, 'It is a fear-ful thing to fall into the hands of the living God'.

Even given what seems like a natural vocation for the spiritual, none the less your composing career has taken a long time to explore many avenues which in retrospect you have come to regard as inadequate modes of musical composition.

With hindsight, I can see that that is the case, although it seems to me that it has just come upon me, as it were. Maybe I was just conscious of the true situation but I couldn't have articulated it at the time I wrote pieces like, for instance, *Ultimos Ritos*, *Thérèse*, *The Whale* and *Celtic Requiem*. But looking back I see I was not happy, basically. Not that 'happy' is a word that I would apply to my life; rather I was not at peace with myself. Now I am much more at peace with myself, because I totally believe that the only way to write music is for the music to be revealed. An eschatological dimension begins to well up inside me.

Listening to works like Celtic Requiem *and* Ultimos Ritos, *one can sense, in the way in which they seek to burst the bounds of convention, the search for something beyond the mere business of fabricating human music. There is a sort of nascent meta-physics almost from the beginning.*

When the BBC put on the festival of my works in London for my fiftieth birthday, I hadn't heard *Ultimos Ritos* for many years. I went to it expecting to be as struck as I always was by it, but I was frankly disappointed, because in the same festival they were per-forming works that I'd written more recently, and there I could actually see the difference between the Western, the much more exterior and formalistic approach of my earlier compositions. This formalism absolutely precludes what the Orthodox call 'the gift of tears'. When I listen to some of my recent pieces like *Res-urrection*, *The Apocalypse*, *Akathist of Thanksgiving*, or any of the recent shorter pieces like *Agraphon* or *Eternity's Sunrise*, *Eonia*, *The Lamb* or *Song for Athene* and things like *As One*

Who Has Slept, my reaction to such pieces very often brings 'the gift of tears'. These pieces seem to be in contact with an intuitive metaphysical dimension that I'm sure a poet like Dante must have been in touch with. And without question Romanos the Melodist brings the gift of tears. It's the same with Indian sacred music and the music of the Sufis. It does not set up limits. It is fully inclusive, never exclusive. It does not organize things in a human fashion. It helps everyone to find their true self.

When was the earliest appearance in your work of these meta-physical concerns?
I can see it very faintly in the first of the Donne Sonnets, which I wrote when I was fifteen. I think after that I lost it for quite a while. I knew nothing about metaphysics in those days so it must have been present at a subliminal level in that Donne Sonnet. It manifests itself, I think, in the spacing and the use of chords to represent certain things. And generally the very slow pacing of the music. It's one of the works that I look back to with most pleasure, even though I'm looking back forty years.

Is there a work in which you feel you made your farewell to the concert hall and began to embody 'liquid metaphysics' in your music?
I think it must have been in what I consider one of my most rad-ical pieces: *Prayer for the World.* But this music was in between two worlds. I would call it my intellectual asceticism – I was still working with complex matrixes of notes and yet at the same time I was concentrating on divesting myself of the materiality of 'note structures'. I suppose in those years I did serve the 'god of philosophers' who does not really exist. In *Prayer for the World* I only partially experienced spiritual liberty.

Were you aware, in writing it, that you were opening up a new dimension of music?
I wasn't very confident in those days, but I realized I was doing a very extreme and possibly important thing. Although I had to

ring people up and say, 'What did you think?', most of them
said, 'I couldn't make head or tail of it.' But on the other hand,
several times in my life, people have told me that I could go no
further in marrying music and spirituality. For instance, at the
time of writing *Coplas*, the head of the Cheltenham Festival told
me that although this piece went deep, I simply could not go any
further. However, at a later stage, when I read St Simeon the
New Theologian and St Ephrem, I was already taken further by
them in the marriage of music and metaphysics – now the possibilities of this marriage seem endless.

*So you're not pursuing a linear development in your music, writ-
ing one piece and then considering the next piece as a development from that. It's really a process of finding in each work the
perfect incarnation from an eternal centre?*
You could say it's a sort of musical process towards becoming
music. But also becoming the ethos of the early Fathers of the
Church, the masters. And finally, I suppose, in our affliction we
open ourselves for a response – a revelation – coming from Him.

Because I don't know how else to express it, I often put on my
scores words like 'beyond compassion that we can comprehend'
instead of 'allegro moderato', or I give just a metronome mark-
ing. I put above the top 'beyond tenderness'; 'so tender that it's
beyond any compassion that we can imagine'. So a lot of direc-
tions for singing or playing my music and indicating something of
the style in which it should be performed are added in somewhat
poetic language. Sometimes I take expressions of the Fathers and
put them over the top. And then usually people say, 'Well, John,
what do you mean by that?' And then I try to explain.

*So you are pushing your performers to go beyond the conven-
tional limits of music-making and in a sense challenging them
spiritually?*
Challenging them to 'theologize' their music-making. But it
depends on the performer or performers. I recall telling Steven
Isserlis to play *The Protecting Veil* like a Byzantine nobleman

who is in exile, but who is very happy about it. Now, although Steven is, on the surface, a clown, deep down he understands intuitively what I am saying. So when I say that I am challenging performers to 'theologize' their music-making, I cannot possibly actually ask them to do so unless I know that I am on very safe ground. So I use images.

I remember telling the players of the Helsinki Philharmonic Orchestra to play with more of the joy of 'Pascha', which in Greek and Russian means 'Easter'. And since much of Finland is Orthodox I thought they would understand. There was an ominous silence and then subdued giggling – in Finnish, 'Pascha' means 'shit'. So one must tread warily, even with the images. Also 'inward' and 'esoteric' are totally different concepts. 'Inward' applies to Germanic humanism, while 'esoteric' relates to the sacred.

You have used the words 'exoteric' and 'esoteric' in speaking of your music; you spoke of the sayings of the Fathers and the way in which you add instructions to your scores. Such things are a long way from the expectations of the average concert-goer who, more or less, has to accept a whole convention of music-making and appreciation that is far from your ideal. Perhaps as a contribution to our understanding of that ideal we can explore these two concepts. Your use of the words 'esoteric' and 'exoteric' suggests that tradition is working in your music in a symbolical sense.

Take, for instance, a piece like *Ultimos Ritos*, where tradition functions in a very exoteric and very Western way. The disposition of the instruments, the fact that timpani are placed in all four corners of the cathedral, the fact that the choir is in cruciform formation, the fact that, at a section in this piece which I call Descent of the Eucharist, trumpets represent the instruments of royalty and the fact that they're echoed by flutes from on high which represent Divine Love: this whole disposition of the forces is a very exoteric way of using traditional elements and it remains, I would say, a theology imposed from the outside.

By contrast, the most esoteric way I have ever proceeded is in a piece like *Mystagogia*, where I'm hardly able to tell where the notes have come from at all. It's almost as if the compositional process itself formed a *via negativa* that grew out of a text I did not set but had in my mind.

I suppose another example of an exoteric way of music-making for you is the use of Bach material in some of your works?
Yes, because Bach is not 'the sacred'. You can use him as a symbol of the religious, but he's not truly sacred. I have used him as a symbol, in an exoteric way, in *Ultimos Ritos* and in *Introit for St John Damascene*. I was putting my own music to sleep, as it were. These were the beginnings of trying to find a metaphysical language. Also, once you start to think too hard, then all sorts of mental processes get in the way. I go back to St Gregory Nazianzen, who said that what is not spontaneous does not exist at all. When I was writing *Ultimos Ritos* I was using formulae, but this was still exoteric, because I was using Bach material as a formula, to take over my own music – that's another formula. I was also using a matrix of notes, even though they were based on the Bach Crucifixus – that's also an exoteric formula. Messiaen, I think, is a supreme example of a modern composer who never really goes beyond the exoteric. Yet I have to concede that that is the Western way of doing things. It is incomprehensible to me that any composer who is concerned with the sacred should proceed in such a way.

Both you and Messiaen have used Hindu rhythms – what's the difference? Would you say your use of Hindu rhythms is exoteric, or esoteric?
I'd like to think it was esoteric because whenever I have used Hindu rhythms there is a metaphysical reason for it.

I wrote a piece that was almost totally within the Indian tradition, called *Samaveda* (1997), using Indian instruments and an Indian singer, Patricia Rozario. That used aspects of *dhrupad* style.

But a more interesting example would be a piece I'm working on at the moment, *Zoë*, which refers to life eternal. The music for Christ is based on the highly complex rhythms of Samavedic chant. I always find it very difficult to write music for Christ, because in many ways Christ is often speaking in a very esoteric language.

In another piece, *The Last Discourse* (1997), where Christ talks to his disciples just before his crucifixion, He's speaking entirely to them and one does not know whether even they understand Him. For instance, Christ says things like 'For a while I go away from you'; 'In my Father's house are many mansions'; 'Where I go you cannot come'. It seems like an intensely esoteric language and I had to find a musical equivalent. It is not up to us composers to make a superficial joining of elements of different religions. But what I think we can do, certainly from a musical point of view, is to use an 'obscure' musical language for the voice of Christ. In *The Last Discourse* I use a severely microtonal *dhrupad*-like melodic line for the music of Christ, and the effect was referred to as being not of this world. In *Zoë* I use Samavedic rhythms, which (as I have said before) are impossibly difficult to notate and difficult to sing because of the endless differing tempi of each bar. As we speak I haven't heard it. But I hope it will convey this obscure, rather awesome tone to Christ's utterances.

So, as the word implies, the exoteric is on the outside, it's something superimposed upon the music for purposes of compositional procedure and performance. And, again, as the word implies, the esoteric is on the inside. It's not to do with the compositional and performance procedures but to do with the inner disposition of both the composer and the performer to the spiritual and metaphysical content of the music.

Yes. And I might add that the esoteric has taken a very, very long time to grow in me. I'd be hard pushed to say in which piece of music I was aware of the esoteric appearing for the first time. All I can say is that it has something to do with lack of labour, 'lack

of earthly care', with total, total subjection to the word of God.
I don't want to sound over-pious here but it requires a humility
to acknowledge that everything I've learnt up to this point is
mediocre and pretty useless, but now I want to go further. I want
to forget everything I have learned. I want something new to
take over. It is like a flame, and the flame of this love draws the
mind wholly into the heart, where it merges into one with the
heart. At least that is what I pray will happen.

Is esotericism for you wholly non-Western?
Well, I've not come across truly esoteric music in any Western
music that I've heard, with the possible exception, I suppose, of
Gregorian chant. But even Gregorian chant (well, I would say
this, wouldn't I? I'm Orthodox) always sounds to me like a
rather feeble version of Byzantine chant. As I have said, the
Western Church turns to the world, whereas the Orthodox
Church always turns towards heaven. You only have to walk
into an Orthodox church – the shape of it, the architecture of it
– and you will find that it doesn't do any 'aspiring', unlike great
Gothic cathedrals with their enormously high vertical structures. An Orthodox church doesn't do any aspiring. When you
enter it you are already surrounded by ikons of Christ, the
Mother of God, all the saints on frescos all over the dome. They
are all round you. So you're surrounded by heaven.

You're immediately plunged into the divine presence?
You're immediately in the divine presence, yes.

*Whereas in a Gothic cathedral the sacred is always some way
off, it's still to be journeyed to.*
I think this word 'aspiration' is very important, because a Western Christian tends to aspire to God – again, this is a very sweeping generalization – whereas the Eastern Orthodox Christian is
already aware of the divine presence. To an Orthodox, religion
is more about removing the dross that obscures what is already
divine, rather than attaining some distant spiritual goal. You see

it in the whole of Western tradition. Even in composers like Victoria or Palestrina, there is always aspiration. Bach is full of this yearning after the solace of the personal God. But if you listen to the music of the East, somehow the divine is already there. *It is* – which is a parallel with the eternal '*I am*'.

Do you want your audience to be aware of the distinction between exoteric and esoteric?
No, I don't think so. Once the music has left my study it has nothing to do with me.

These distinctions simply help you to focus your musical imagination?
Absolutely. Although people have come up to me after performances of some of the more recent pieces and said, 'I just don't know how or where this music of yours comes from.' I don't know myself, so I can't be much help to them.

This esoteric music that I am struggling to describe to you in words – the esoteric itself doesn't mean that the music is clever, it doesn't mean that it's more beautiful, it certainly doesn't mean that it's more exciting. It speaks of an everlasting and unchanging reality and it exists on a higher plane. It is not subject to human manipulation. Different, higher, elusive by nature, it comes in a different way. The reality of other dimensions tears through the screen of our earthly body, penetrating our feeble nature.

Music and Revelation

JOHN TAVENER: The difficulty in listening to my own music of say twenty or even fifteen years ago is that I'm terribly aware of the impurity of what is simulated in it. For me, this extends to listening to almost all Western music, because of the fact that so much of it is fabricated to flatter the ear. That is why Western music seems, superficially at least, more 'beautiful' in an aesthetic sense, and for that reason far more easy to listen to. Whereas the music that exists for the sake of a higher plane is not music you can just sit down to in the evening and enjoy a glass of wine while you are listening to it. It's music that requires a different kind of attention. The listener has to give himself to the music in an entirely different way.

BRIAN KEEBLE: *In which case, what state of being and what expectations would you like listeners to bring to a performance of your music?*
I can only answer such a question from, as it were, an ideal situation. First of all I do not say 'Do this, do that', 'Listen to this, look out for that'. This is the way of Western classical music.

Rather, I would say: here is something that *is* before all ages coming to birth – something new – something already known. But it is not what *I* have done that is important, rather the spirit that has animated it. Close the mind and open the heart. Expect nothing and you may receive 'something'.

Stockhausen demands what his performers should *look* like, and tells his audience how to react. That is arrogant and Germanic beyond anything I could say. You cannot *tell* people what to do. If they have a reaction – a *metanoia*, even – all well and good. If not – all well and good.

But the look of the space is all important. The average opera house suggests contrivance and artificiality pushed to their limit. The South Bank and the Barbican are for Varèse onwards. People should listen to my music with darkened lighting, or with an ikon and a candle in front of it – perhaps.

We live in a society that is not geared at all to my kind of music, or to a way of thinking that recognizes any hierarchy of values. For me to say music exists for the sake of a higher plane is to risk causing offence and misunderstanding to some people, because audiences today are not attuned to such a way of thinking. But if you said it to an Indian, or a Sufi musician, or to an Orthodox Psaltist, or to an Aborigine, or even an American Indian, I think they would understand exactly what I am trying to convey to you. In the same way that they would not understand at all what a Western man was saying if he said he liked to listen to Elliott Carter, or Boulez, or Birtwistle, because it 'gives you something to get your teeth into'. Who wants to get their teeth into a piece of music? Music is to glorify God. That's all.

But the way you conceive of and compose music does rather presuppose that the listener can and must enter into a more objective state of being, a state of being where personal emotions and appetites are not aroused for the sake of it. But the paradox is, of course, that in composing music at all you must at least want to engage with the personal response of the listener. Are you aware of this paradox?

Yes, I am, but I think to write music in which, as it were, one's own personality has become transparent, one has to become in oneself a saint first, and I'm certainly not a saint. Only the Masters – Romanov the Melodist, Rumi the Sufi poet, come to mind – finally achieve this. I think the ego does disappear if you have given yourself up totally to the spiritual life.

In my case music is always ahead of what spiritual state I'm in: my music is always ahead of me. The music guides me and tells me things about myself which could not be made clear to me in any other way. Moreover, you cannot teach this way of writing music. It's something that comes from deep inside one and takes one by surprise, quite honestly. I'm not aware of any conscious deliberation while I'm at work. For me, it's just a void, and each new piece is a new beginning.

Perhaps the idea I had in mind – to do with getting rid of the ego – was ill-chosen, and a better way of approaching the question would be to think in terms of the whole ethos of humility?
Yes, I think you're right. But that does not mean I'm a particularly humble person. It's the humility to be able to receive, and to forget what I personally think, or what I personally might like to do, or my personal aggression or my personal anything.

A humility linked to courage, because, as you have often said, we have to have the courage to admit that we don't know, in the face of the awesome mystery of God.
Precisely because one is plunging into an abyss, and we do not know what we're going to find there.

On the other hand, of course, it feels like the most natural thing in the world when it does happen. By that, I mean it feels most in accord with our own being, it has a beauty beyond beauty, it has a transcendence almost beyond transcendence, it has a joy beyond joy. Any adjective you can think of, it's beyond it. And it feels natural, absolutely natural – just as natural as it would be for me to go outside now, look at a tree or see the sky – which of course in itself is a miracle anyway. It doesn't feel miraculous, it feels as though that is the norm. At the time I'm not thinking, my God, what an extraordinary thing is happening. It just happens.

Does what you have just said presuppose that such music as you hope will be 'given' to you will be simple music?
I've used the word 'transparent'. It has to be transparent and its transparency consists in what is *not* there – it's almost as if what is not there is the divine silence. Does that make sense?

Coming back to the question of what is natural in this apparently supernatural environment or state, when I venerate the bones of a saint, it's always accompanied by the sweet smell of paradise. And that seems the most normal and natural thing in the world. I would say that when I write a piece like *Eternity's Sunrise* or *Mystagogia*, I don't appear to be doing any thinking about it myself, it seems the most natural thing in the world – as natural as breathing.

In the past poets and artists spoke of having a muse, and of course one associates the muse with the feminine. Do you have a specific sense of the 'feminineness' of your creative energies?
A supreme example of the feminine principle in this respect is Sophia, Holy Wisdom; in Christian terms, the Mother of God. There was a time a few years ago when I thought all my best music was written about the Mother of God, not because I have read theological books about her, but simply because I love her. The feminine is something which is largely absent from our times. It's got distorted, contorted by feminism. I am talking about reinstating the sacred, feminine principle back into art.

I remember a very simple, humble priest preaching a sermon – I thought he put it wonderfully. He said, 'Unless we have first become the Mother of God, then we cannot bear Christ within us.' I've always remembered that, because it was such a wonderfully simple way of putting it. I love Byzantine chant because of its certitude, because of its utter adherence to the Word. But it is very masculine. But then in the richness of Orthodoxy, if you listen to Znamenny or Russian chant, you're aware of its feminine counterpart.

It's the same as with good and evil. In a piece like *The Apocalypse*, when I tried to represent evil – I mean, evil as such. The Devil cannot create, so all I could do was invert the material, or pervert the material, if you like, pour ink over it, smudge it. But better still, more traditionally, invert it. Anyway, I know that in my own music, if the feminine and masculine do not co-exist, then it's not balanced.

I suppose in *The Apocalypse* – it's such a mighty subject – perhaps the masculine slightly dominates. But if we are to go on considering the masculine and the feminine, my music tends generally to be feminine. But then if you look at the Byzantine Church, that is feminine. All this nonsense about feminine priests! For a start we have Sophia, the Sophianic principle, almost totally unknown in the West; secondly we have the Mother of God; thirdly, just look at the architecture. The architecture of a beautiful, small Byzantine church is feminine. It's in the shape of a breast: the dome. We have none of these masculine spires.

What do you say to the suggestion that you really ought to be writing liturgical music?
First of all, who wants it? Secondly, I'm certainly *not* writing liturgical music. It may be music that has been influenced by liturgical music; the form may have some connection with liturgical music. *The Apocalypse* certainly has liturgical elements to it, but a piece like *Mystagogia*, although it may well be based on a liturgical 'secret' acting as a sub-structure (no one would ever be able to tell that), the music seems to be coming from nowhere. Maybe it's closer to the revealed truths that came to the early Desert Fathers, the Egyptian Desert Fathers. Maybe it harks back to a time before any formalized mode of worship existed. I can only say maybe – I haven't a clue. Maybe it is a primordial music that harks back to a time before churches and the putting together of liturgies.

It might help if I give a very parable-like response. It relates to how the funeral service of the Orthodox Church actually came into being. In the very early centuries there was a writer and composer known as St John of Damascus and for a time he'd not written anything. This didn't bother him very much – he just got on with praying and doing the rest of the things that a monk does. But when one of the brethren died, whom he must have loved very much, he spontaneously sang and 'received' the words for what has become the Orthodox Funeral Service. It may sound very arrogant of me to say that the act of composition is for me something similar; at least that's how it feels.

One of the most obvious uses of tradition in your music is that of the eight tones of Byzantine chant. How do you see your use of these tones in your own music?
I have contemplated Byzantine tones rather than studied them in any academic way. I haven't read vast treatises on Byzantine tones. I have contemplated them so that they have become part of me and I have become part of them. It's a very interesting fact that the Byzantines decided that there should be just eight tones. Whereas in India there are probably up to ninety tone systems. There is a great similarity between the Byzantine tones and the Indian tone system. (I wish somebody would write a book on the subject.) At a certain point in history the Church decided to limit the tones to eight.

Having got to how many?
Well, I think there were well over a hundred. There was just so much music that they had to limit it. Also, there was a Pythagorean theory behind this use of only eight tones. They were written for each day of the week and the eighth tone was meant to represent eternity.

What were the origins of these tones?
It was a mixture of Plato, Pythagoras and the music written for the Synagogue during the earthly Incarnation of Christ, all put together, each tone representing a different spiritual state.
I would say that all the chant I'm talking about is revealed, and I'm sure the way that tones were put together was also revealed – it cannot be any other way. If you speak of Plato, that is revealed truth; if you talk about Pythagoras, I would say that is revealed truth; if you talk about music for the Synagogue, that is revealed truth. Possibly I'm wrong, but I believe that chant, whether it be Indian or whether it be Byzantine or whatever it may be, is the nearest we can get to the music that was

breathed into man when God created the world. I see it in that light. I don't see how, by the use of any human contrivance, you could arrive at something like chant. A Greek would argue that Byzantine chant is in the apostolic tradition and therefore could go no further. Nothing else could happen to it, and it comes straight down from the time of Christ, because it was the music He heard in the synagogue.

Now linked to this is the concept that Christ has always existed ('Before Abraham was, I am'). This ever-present reality of Christ is all important. At the time of Plato, Christ existed. All through the Old Testament, Christ existed. In other words, Christ existed before the world existed. So this omnipresence of Christ throughout all time is reflected in the way these tones are put together.

A Greek would probably also argue that other systems couldn't come into existence; they can only be Greek tone systems because they are based on the apostolic tradition. But I would argue with that and say that the Byzantine tones as sung today have been bastardized by both Syriac usage and Turkish influence. We don't know how close they are to what they were originally; therefore there's no reason why they shouldn't be used in order to reveal a tone system to another country, as they did to Russia. There must be a different tone system for every country, that is part of Orthodoxy. We do not have a sacred language in the sense of Latin in the Roman Catholic Church. Indeed, if anything the language should be Greek. But both the music and the language must be understood by the particular country.

If England were to become an Orthodox country, someone – I suppose it would be me, I can't think of anyone else at the moment – would have to start in a very simple way composing tones for the English Orthodox Church. In those circumstances I might take as a kind of a prototype the Byzantine, parts of the Slavonic, parts of Znamenny, parts of the Syriac, parts of the Coptic or Celtic. And I repeat, I believe that all chant in great traditions stems from the very first breath of God.

So your immersion in the tones places you in the proper tradition and metaphysical context for you to compose music that has an authentic and legitimate spiritual dimension?

Yes, and, in a sense, the *only* context, because if someone asks me to write a piece about, for instance, the Ascension or the Falling Asleep of the Mother of God, I would have to know the prototype, the archetype, before beginning to write a single note. The fact that I know what it is in all eight tones is not a guarantee of writing sacred music. It cannot be a matter of superficial copying, but rather a total assimilation of the sacred tones which in turn become the foundation of a musical language.

But, as I have said, it is not my wish to compose liturgical music. Rather to show what I have learned from it; that things present and things to come are made clear in musical terms. Not discursively, obviously, but by their being made manifest – a theophany, a revelation of man and God. Whether I succeed, it is not for me to judge.

You've referred to eight Byzantine tones. What is the significance of each of these tones?

They refer to different spiritual states, rather in the way that Indian ragas refer to spiritual states. The eight tones express the pain and suffering of Holy Week and the joy of the Resurrection. There is nothing that strikes a false note. In the eight tones everything is lit by another, uncreated light, and the faithful see everything with other spiritual senses.

Do you think the tones, as they operate in your music, might eventually have the same effect on an audience?

If at all, only subliminally. And I think I have to cling on to the word 'subliminally'. We live in a world that knows nothing about these things. But I am optimistic about any intuitive response, which I must say I get much of the time. After all, there's no reason why passengers have to know how to fly a plane: they are happy if they arrive safely. If my music can communicate subliminally, then I can only say that I am humbled and happy.

What seems to have emerged from our discussion of the role of tradition and metaphysics in your music is that these do not supply you with either a formula or a set of criteria by which you might go about the composition of a piece of music.

That's absolutely right. They don't give any formulae. In some ways they don't give anything in a formal way. They are something that I imbibe. With each new piece of music I have no idea whether it's going to continue or what it's going to do. There is not even the possibility that I'm necessarily going to write another piece of music. You have to rely totally on faith, and faith in tradition, which basically is faith in God – I don't see any difference between the two. When tradition reaches the level I've been talking about, tradition and faith are the same thing. Which doesn't guarantee a thing. It certainly does not guarantee that I am going to write anything that's any good.

Plenty of things come apparently out of heaven and they're dreadful! But at its best, when tradition is really working inside me in the way wine ferments, then I would risk being blasphemous by saying that the act of composing is a sacrament.

Shaping the Resonances

We all have been parts of Adam, we have heard those melodies in Paradise. Although the water and earth of our bodies have caused a doubt to fall upon us, something of those melodies comes back to our memory.

Rumi

BRIAN KEEBLE: *I've heard you describe the act of composition as a sort of 'non-physical martyrdom'. Can you explain?*

JOHN TAVENER: I've thought a lot about this. When I made that remark it was against the background of the fact that I was clearly swimming against the tide to such a degree that everything I was dealing with was against modern life. Actually it was Mother Thekla who said to me that 'composing for you is an act of martyrdom'. I've thought more and more about it since then and the thought I had recently was that at the point of writing, the point of actually composing or re-creating, or better still, copying God's work, one is incredibly near the prototype, or, if you like, one is very near God. At that point, if someone came into the room and told me that I could not write, then I think I would be prepared to die for that. It's as if (without being blasphemous) when the spoon containing Holy Communion is about to touch your tongue, for that one second you are actually in eternity, and if somebody cuts you off and tells you that you can't receive it, then you will be prepared to die.

I recall that when I married for the first time, Metropolitan Anthony said, 'If you truly love someone, you will be prepared to die for them, and to say "I love you" is tantamount to saying you are ready to die.' Seen from the same perspective, an artist, at that brief moment of contact with the prototype or with God, must be prepared to lay down his life if somebody tries to stop him working.

Then, from what you have said, not to work must be a sort of hell?
Yes, it feels as if the umbilical cord has been broken between this world and the next. For me, to work is to pray. One's whole life is a prayer, therefore not to work is hell. At the moment of that actual meeting of the prototype or the meeting with God, you could say, just for that split second, 'I *know* that God exists.' However, if I'm at some frivolous party and somebody comes up and asks me, do I know if God exists, of course I don't know if God exists. I'm not a saint. Only at that split second when one's writing does one know it. In a way one is in a different realm, totally cut off from the world, outside in this act of re-creation. I use that word as the more I think about writing music, the more and more it seems like looking and looking and looking at God, and then copying his work. 'The work has been done – now glorify.'

There is something mysterious about this moment. To describe it makes it sound as if it's a moment of time, but really it's the moment that puts you out of time.
Yes, it's a moment outside time. Absolutely.

The mechanical part of your writing takes place in the flow of time, but the essence of your energies that seek to realize the work is outside the flow of time. In the modern world, work and prayer are hardly considered to be connected at all. But in the traditional context, of course, work and prayer are two faces of the same state of being. How do you prepare for a new work?
As the Fathers say, 'To him who knows himself is given knowledge of all things. For knowing yourself is the fulfilment of the knowledge of all things.' So I know what I have to write, not by thought, but by intuition working through experience.

None the less, you have been fortunate in that what you have written, shall we say, 'of necessity', has always been accepted as commissioned work. In view of the fact that external, circumstantial stimulus means so little to you, do you have a fear of drying up?
Not now. Not for the last twenty years or so. When I was younger and was composing using fabricated techniques and formulae, I often wondered whether I'd ever write again. Now I think it's more a question of how many years do I have left to live – because of this heart problem – and will I have enough time to actually write out what is inside me? But it doesn't ultimately matter and it's certainly none of my business.

From the way you've talked about your music so far, perhaps it's easier to understand your inner motivation to 're-create'. But even so, what external things might *spark your imagination?*
I should say that anything could spark me off, because I'm in a very vulnerable state when I'm beginning to feel around for sound, for music. It could be a text, it could be unrelated, just a few groups of notes that I happen to hear from a distance. I remember once, at my house in Sussex, I heard some chanting and I thought, where on earth is this coming from? I went out in the car and finally traced it: it was coming from a Jewish wedding. The music I heard from the distance, I had already sketched out; when I actually got to the wedding the chanting had finished. But that gives an example.

On a more specific level, I suppose the sound of the Dagar Brothers has influenced me, or the sound of that 'nightingale of Mount Athos', Father Fifiris. He is dead now but his highly ornate and deeply microtonal singing (on records) is miraculous and should be listened to by anyone who has an ear. His phenomenal control, his endless wavering between pitches – it comes closest, in my experience, to the ecstatic song of the nightingale, but of course at a very much lower pitch. Even when he was over ninety you could feel or sense all the microtones between the notes. But he was unique in Byzantine music and I count myself lucky to have heard him.

Recently you've spoken of being impressed by the timbres of early instruments of the Academy of Ancient Music.
I certainly have. I would like to collaborate with them and I want to write more music for them. First of all, I prefer the more sober sound of the Academy of Ancient Music to the rather brash sound of the modern symphony orchestra.

But one of the most important things that my meeting with this group has brought forth is something very surprising, because at the age of fifty-five I had begun to think I was beyond being influenced by anything; I had nothing more to be taught. But I've started listening to Handel's oratorios and operas, *Solomon, Saul, Judas Maccabaeus, Belshazzar, Semele, Israel in Egypt, Theodora* and *Jephtha*, played on period instruments, and I was absolutely stunned by this music. It was the spontaneity of Handel, the spontaneity of his invention, the fact that he does not develop; in the way he might start a fugue and then immediately cut it off with another incredibly striking idea. And it's so simple, so beautiful. Listen to a piece like *Solomon*, the second aria, sung by Solomon's wife, it's surely one of the most deeply feminine pieces of music ever written. Listen to the farewell song of the Queen of Sheba – again one of the greatest and noblest valedictory songs ever written. With the flick of a pen he evokes the locusts in *Israel in Egypt*. The whole last act of *Saul* strikes me as reaching a level of almost Sophoclean tragedy. And the music of *Jephtha* – of Jephtha himself and the exquisite music written for his daughter Isis who is to be sacrificed. This music brings tears to my eyes. Handel is indeed the master of us all – certainly in terms of Western classical music.

One could say that Bach is much more profound, but if I want profundity I would go to Byzantine or Znamenny chant. In one sense I don't actually *need* Bach, but I still listen to a cantata a day. Handel fascinates me more. Recently I played to myself on the piano the whole of the first act of Mozart's *The Marriage of Figaro* and I thought, yes, yes, in its own humanistic terms it's perfect, but it's still cerebral. Of course Bach is cerebral, and Handel is not. Handel can be routine and uninspired – in his concerti grossi – but when he's at his best he absolutely stuns me. Every night now I sit with a glass of wine and explore Handel's operas and oratorios.

What about Handel in relation to your own music?
I haven't experienced anything quite like this meeting with Handel since I had that extraordinary revelation when I was twelve and heard Stravinsky's *Canticum Sacrum* and Mozart's *Magic Flute*. But undoubtedly Handel is 'sinking in' – it takes a long time for any influence to show, but I think he still has things to teach me. For instance, his masterly unbroken melodic sense. He never reminds one of the powdered wig, in the way that Mozart does in something like *The Marriage of Figaro*. I know Mozart transcends the powdered wig, but you're much more aware of the frivolous age in which he lived with Mozart than you are with Handel. There is some music of mine that I'm thinking of at this very moment as I speak, and I realize that a kind of 'petrified' Handel could find its way to influence it. By this, I mean that the miraculous beauty of Handel's music is somehow taken out of time and frozen into an ecstatic eternal present. He's the only composer of the past, or the present, who has actually stimulated me in this way.

Perhaps it's not that difficult to imagine how a work like The Lamb, *or a short choral piece, can come to you complete. But what happens when you are working on a much larger piece?*
That depends on what the work is. If it has a text, and if the text is compiled by Mother Thekla, it's usually the text that will start me off. But if it's a very long work, then the last thing I do is sit at a desk, staring at the text and thinking, oh my God, how am I going to do this? If I do that and I feel there is a difficulty and I begin to feel the dreaded existential angst, then I know I'm on the wrong path. If I have to work at something too hard, I know that either the idea is wrong, or the text is wrong, or the thing just has to be thrown out.

Basically it's a question of living with the text over a period of weeks, maybe months, doing other things – buying fish, choosing wine, driving the car, going for a walk. If I was fit enough to garden, I'd do so. It's a bit like the Buddhist idea of planting a tree in order to concentrate the mind, by doing something very simple. All during this time the notes and patterns of notes are beginning to form in my head. I don't know where they come from. I try to delay the time of actually writing it down because I'm never quite sure when I've finally reached the point where it's possible to commit ideas to paper. Also the old Adam, the laziness in me, sometimes wins over, and the prospect of having to work on a piece of music for the next six months or whatever it is, makes me want to put it off as long as I can. But if the music has a text, then I will probably start much quicker.

Do you set yourself specific hours in the day to work?
When I'm driving, walking or whatever, of course I don't. But I might just come up to my studio and look at whatever I've sketched every day and maybe one extra little idea will come to me during the day and I'll note it down. But when I finally start to write the whole piece, then it comes very quickly, because it's been simmering, as it were, rather like wine when it's fermenting. Then I go into another state while I'm actually writing.

Do you work on one piece at a time?
Sometimes it's only one, but it might be as many as four. There's no rule.

Many composers use the piano for purposes of composition. Do you?
Yes. In the early stages it is absolutely vital that I use the piano. But possibly only in the early stages. Because once I have the precise sound in my head, I don't need the piano any more. When I bought my house in Greece I thought I might do without one. But I found I had to have one in order to check the sound. Anybody overhearing me compose would probably only hear a few

notes every day. It would just be in order to check. I don't like being overheard. At least, I always thought I did not like being overheard, yet on one occasion there was a party going on behind me while I was working, my own children with Greek children babbling away in Greek, screaming, shouting, and I just went on writing. So I can completely shut myself away from the outside world.

You leave the piano when the work begins to take on a life of its own?
Yes, once I've started 're-creating' – as I've said, I prefer to think of it as that rather than as composing. I only need the piano when I'm not sure about the exact pitches, the exact octaves in which things should come and all the rest of it. Beyond that, the work itself, as it were, tends to tell me what to do.

It can be quite stimulating if I am writing for instruments that I have never written for, as I am at the moment. I'm writing for viols, but to get hold of a viol player at eleven or twelve o'clock at night in Greece, in order to consult them, is extremely difficult. But if I want an answer I usually want it there and then, and I'll go on trying probably till two in the morning and quite ruthlessly wake someone up until I get what I need. Mother Thekla has said to me, 'You don't give a damn about anything or anyone in the whole world when you're writing, you are a totally ruthless tyrant!'

What tells you if something is going wrong with your music? Can you tell by looking at it whether it's right or wrong?
Yes, I can, and not only by looking at the music. It could be by looking at the cat, which I know sounds ridiculous, but there is something deeply mysterious about cats. I think they 'know' things that we don't have access to.

It's the same with landscape; in particular the Greek landscape, about which we've already spoken. When I'm composing in Greece, to walk along and sit by the sea at night or to look at the landscape somehow tells me whether I've got it right or wrong. Sometimes when I look at an ikon of Christ or the Mother of God it has the same effect. I think of the music and I look at the ikon and there's some kind of mysterious inner connection, as there is with the landscape and the cat. Though I must say that in recent years the occasions when I get it wrong seem to be less and less.

This is a very extraordinary thing to say – that you can look at a landscape or an ikon or a cat and somehow tell that the music is right or wrong. Obviously this is a deeply intuitive process. Has this got something to do with the fact that looking at an ikon or a landscape or a cat induces in you a certain state of harmony which you are then able to, as it were, turn to the work itself, to see whether it resonates truly or not?

That's near to it. The use of the word 'resonate' is particularly important. It seems to be a process where one mystery resonates with another. I think that would be the closest I could get to it. If I'm not aware of this process, then I've got it wrong. It would be no use anybody else telling me whether I've got it right or wrong. The process is really beyond such judgements. After all, in a sense, when one is looking at a landscape one is looking at God in the landscape; when one is looking at an ikon, one is looking at God, and it is the same with a cat. So, rather than getting down piously on one's knees and praying, this resonating process is another kind of prayer.

Schoenberg could conceive a work as a whole and then he could sit and watch the television while he was scoring it. I imagine this would be anathema to you. I mean the compositional procedure of conceiving a work and then sitting rather mechanically and orchestrating it.

That would be total anathema to me, because I do not work like Schoenberg. Schoenberg was working with man-made procedures, his own procedures in fact, and I can understand that he could watch the television while he was writing a piece of music, because he knew exactly what he was going to do – because of the formulae. Also, some composers – Maxwell Davies, for instance – seem to know years ahead what work they will be writing. For me, it's inconceivable to plan ahead in that way. I've no idea what I'll be doing at any time in the future – let alone whether I shall be alive. I don't know what is going to come next – I never do know; it's just like entering a new world. Every time.

Can we assume, then, that there is no division for you between conceiving a piece of music and then scoring it?
There is no division, because the music comes already scored. I never have to think what instrument plays this or what instrument plays that. The music comes to me already embodied in instrumental sounds.

You've said you work in pencil. Do you write the score out in full as you go along?
I scribble – I wouldn't say I write it out; I scribble it out in full. I must know roughly what the duration is, and also I must know how I'm going to end it, although sometimes the ending will change during the writing. But I must have a very rough sketch, probably only understandable by myself, from which to work.

So the end point is really more a point of orientation?
When I speak of an ending, I have in mind a metaphysical meaning as the 'end'. It's never a musical one, like: am I going to end on C sharp, am I going to end on G flat, or am I going to end on a high or low note? The important part of how I'm going to end is what I wish to convey metaphysically. Usually there's an element of not knowing at the end, because I feel once a person thinks they know something you can be quite sure they know nothing. In other words, I always end on a musical equivalent of 'not knowing'. How dreadful it would be if we suddenly thought we knew something. We would surely stop altogether?

So you have a sense of moving to a goal, but what the final goal is is an open thing?
Yes, totally . . .

It's not something that you've concluded, something you've made your mind up about?
Absolutely not at all. The use of the word 'goal' gives me the willies, because that suggests something predetermined and for that reason is unsympathetic to me. The way you can feel Beethoven has reached the goal at the end of one of his symphonies, which in a sense you've already anticipated, that's foreign to me.

What about tempo markings?
Tempo markings are important to me. I don't know whether it is the case with other composers, but certainly my own music is always related to the speed of my heartbeat, which is considerably slowed down because of the medication I'm on. I have the heartbeat of an athlete – very slow, somewhere between 40 and 50. That does not necessarily mean that all my music moves at a colossally slow speed. If I am using demi-, semiquavers or whatever, it is always related to the 40 or the 50. Because I have had heart surgery and have a leaking aortic valve I live with the permanent sound of my heartbeat, asleep or awake.

We've talked elsewhere about your need to have, in one sense or another, a text to help your creative energies to flow. In a work like Resurrection, *for instance, we would obviously be referring to an explicit text that can be followed by the audience, and is followed by you in the process of composition. But in a work like* The Protecting Veil, *for instance, there is an implicit text, almost a secret text, which your creative imagination follows at the time of writing but which is not necessary for the audience. In such a case it's almost as if we are referring to programme music. What's the difference?*
It has nothing to do with programme music at all. It's entirely to

do with a metaphysical subtext, which I do not think is necessary for the audience to know. In a piece like *The Protecting Veil*, or much more extremely in a piece like *Mystagogia*, the text is all important to me when I'm working in my studio. But once it's gone outside the studio I cannot dictate to people what they're supposed to think when they're hearing the music.

Does the function of a metaphysical subtext ever pose technical problems with notation?
More and more. The more I've become saturated with traditional music, the more and more difficult it becomes to notate it, because the modern Western way of notating music has precious little to do with the Byzantine neumes or the great oral traditions of India. At the moment I find I have to write out incredibly complicated bars, which don't add up. But perish the day when I have to use actual Byzantine notation – it would give my publishers a major heart attack.

How do you get round these problems? With microtones, for instance?
I have devices. For microtones, my editor Rosalind Mascall and I discuss it. Let's say that there are four microtones between a semitone, then I usually write a half flat with one line through it – that's one degree; if it's two degrees, I write a half flat with two lines through it; if it's three degrees, I do a half, or it might be sharp, then I write a half sharp with four lines through it, etc., etc. One has to invent these things, because they don't exist in Western notation.

What about when you're writing a piece that's been influenced by, or resonates with (or whatever you might call it) Samavedic rhythms, for instance?
The notation of those rhythms is so complicated that I just simply have to write out as nearly as I can what I hear, even though it will not make any sort of sense in terms of a real bar. I almost always explain, by putting a note in the score, that the singer of

this should go and study with an Indian master; and if there's a section which is much indebted to Byzantine chant then I would suggest that the singer go and study with a psaltist. I put it on the score because, obviously, there will come a time when I will not be alive to give such instructions.

Are aleatoric techniques an option for you?
If the Samavedic rhythm is written in strict bar lines and the tempo changes from bar to bar, no conductor could possibly conduct it. Maybe the accompanying sound underneath the chant could be aleatoric. In which case the conductor would just make gestures when things change or stop in the orchestra, but allow the soloist or whoever it is who is playing or singing these Samavedic rhythms to continue on their own, unconnected, as it were. I don't think even then a conductor could realize a score absolutely, because I'm still talking about working with Western singers or performers.

Every time I've tried to work with a traditional artist it has been a problem. I can remember one occasion, there was an Irish traditional singer, and I sent her a score of *Mary of Egypt* and she said to me about a month later that she had interpreted it in her own way, which was wonderful – it was a marvellous thing, extraordinary. I could just hear my music in it but it was completely different, like an extended improvisation on what I had written. This is my problem in working with traditional singers, whether they be Irish, Iranian, Greek, Indian or Turkish.

Do you foresee a time when you might abandon notation?
There may come a time when I don't want to notate music any more, but I rather doubt it. One has to bear in mind that one lives in the West, so if I want my music to be performed at all, if that marvellous meeting with the prototype happens in a composition then it's pretty mean, pretty hard-hearted of me if I say, well, I'm going to keep it to myself because you won't understand the notation. No, for the moment, I will send the performers off to masters and while I am still alive I can demonstrate

with my very feeble singing voice. Young artists are very quick to pick up things, at a superficial level anyway, then later they may go deeper. That is my experience.

What are the occasions when you would use a traditional singer in a piece?
If, for instance, I'm literally quoting chant, Byzantine chant, or, say, Indian chant, then I would write in the score 'psaltist' and a psaltist would have to be found. In *Fall and Resurrection* I have done that. There's another place where I specify music to be played on the *nāy* or *kaval* and in that case one comes up against a problem. The *nāy* player will only play strictly traditional music.

I once met a *nāy* player from Iran. He played me the most wonderful Sufi music, but when it came to him 'realizing' what I had written, he was somehow unable to do so. Fortunately I knew of someone who had been trained in Egypt, but who also knew Western music and made his own instruments, who could play what I wanted. However, he is unique. What of the future . . .?

Do you prefer to use Western-trained singers and performers and then get them to adapt to your 'traditional' requirements?
Yes, unless I'm quoting absolutely verbatim. Otherwise I use Western-trained performers who have imagination.

Since your music must have a metaphysical basis for you to proceed, how does this relate to the actual elements of music – rhythm, for instance?
There has to be a metaphysical reason for rhythm, unless I'm writing a short piece like *The Lamb* or any kind of short choral piece of up to around ten minutes. Such a piece would then be guided entirely by the text. But when I'm using rhythm in a larger context, I have to think in terms of cosmic rhythms in relation to the underlying pulse of the micro-rhythms of the entire work. Middle Eastern and Eastern music has a much richer language of rhythm for this purpose than the West. For instance,

the rhythms of the Sufis all represent different spiritual states.

When I wrote *Theophany* (1992–3), where I used a bandir drum, I used a Sufi rhythm which came to 33 beats. Here I was using rhythm symbolically. I cannot manufacture rhythm. The kind of manufactured rhythm, say, of *The Rite of Spring*, would be very alien to me. This is the kind of music-making which in my view has passed. I think now there has to be a reason for the rhythm, as there has to be a reason for everything in my music.

Can you be more specific about what you mean by having a metaphysical reason for rhythm?

Using rhythm as part of a symbolic language. In *Resurrection* there are certain rhythms that are used every time the voice of Christ appears, and they are based on various rhythmic variants. There are other rhythms that I use and which help to define what is happening. For instance, in Peter's denial the rhythm and the melody are at that particular point exactly the same as the rhythm and melody of St Mary Magdalen's recognition of the risen Christ when she cries 'Ravoni!', 'Master!' But with Peter the music is full of pathos while in Mary Magdalen the music bubbles up inside her, as it were, and is ecstatic. All the rhythms and all the melodic lines between them are interconnected in a metaphysical pattern. Without this interconnectedness the music is just 'made up' and so without real foundation. Sometimes, however, one can feel oneself to be in a metaphysical 'chaos', with all the symbols. I am thinking here of St Ephrem the Syrian, who said once, while writing his poetry, 'Jesus, you have so many symbols I'm drowning in a sea of them.'

Then, of course, there are other ways of using rhythm; or not using rhythm. Suddenly you expect something to happen. Christ is about to sing and you expect him to make the same sound that he's been making and to use the same rhythms – suddenly you annihilate that rhythm. For instance, at the point on the Cross when he cries, '*Eli, Eli, lama sabachthani*' – 'My God, My God, why has thou forsaken me?' – I deliberately cut what was to be expected in order to shock by this extraordinary statement of Christ. Later on, at the point of the Resurrection itself, the same melody and the same rhythms that Christ had are taken up with everybody sharing in what amounts to a cosmic Resurrection.

What is the metaphysical basis of melody in your work?
It's very similar to that of chant. In works like *Resurrection* or *The Apocalypse* it acts symbolically to help identify the spiritual state that we should be experiencing. For instance, in *The Apocalypse* I use seven tones which represent the Seven Angels of the Apocalypse, the Seven Disasters, etc., etc. So every time something like the Seven Churches comes up, then the melodic line of that particular tone will identify it and connect it with the seven trumpets. Maybe the listener, if he has a good enough ear, will be aware of it subliminally. It's a way of defining (particularly in *The Apocalypse*) good and evil by using different melodies or tones for different spiritual states.

Again, as with chant, I can suddenly dance out of tradition, as it were, maybe to represent 'evil' or silence, and play surrealistic games in order deliberately to confuse or terrify the audience, because it's not what they expect any more. Particularly in *The Apocalypse* and *Resurrection,* there are moments when it is extremely important to turn the melody upside-down, to parody it. In *The Toll Houses* I use a traditional melody, 'Behold the bridegroom comes at midnight; beware lest you find yourselves sleeping'; then, because this is a pantomime about the afterlife taking place in an aerial zoo, when we see the fornicating monkeys the melody of the Bridegroom is turned upside-down into a jazz break.

So, melody is used in order to symbolize – I can't just write any old melody. The only time I can write a spontaneous melody (the same with rhythm) would be in a short pieces like *The Lamb*, *The Tyger, Eonia*, or *As One Who Has Slept*, or of course in that most mysterious piece of all, *Mystagogia*, where I have no idea where anything comes from. There are so many unaccompanied choral pieces where I was guided by the text, and melody simply came out of the text. Sometimes a melody just comes into my head. None the less, it must have a symbolic reason for being there.

So melody and rhythm really come back to the same root?
They have exactly the same root and it's a metaphysical root.

What about the ison *or eternity note?*
The *ison* represents for me the divine presence, and somewhere I suppose in every piece that I write this eternity note must be present – the presence of God, as it were. Unless, again, I want to make a metaphysical point by shocking the audience and then I remove it.

Let's be very specific here: metaphysically the drone is the acoustic representation of silence?
The silence of God. The silence of eternity. Yes.

That which is *before anything is determined by being?*
And when I cut it off, I want to symbolically represent an apparent void.

On that basis, then, it must indicate that the 'events' in your music take place in sacred time?
Yes, that's my intention. It's got nothing to do with historical time.

The audience then, whether it realizes it or not, in sitting through this continuous note, is immersed in the articulation of the eternal, the 'vibration', shall we say, of the eternal?
Indeed, and for Eastern musicians or for Byzantine singers it's a great honour to sing the *ison* or the drone, precisely because it represents the eternal. But Western musicians don't see it this way. And sometimes they complain about having to hold a single note for over two hours. I recall, though, the string quartet in *The Apocalypse* were both understanding and cooperative.

They just complained about the physical pain it gave their hands and arms. And I don't blame them. But of course, for the most part in *The Apocalypse*, you cannot hear them – they are deliberately drowned out and then suddenly you are aware of them again, or of a sudden you are *not* aware of them. And that, I hope the listener notices, is awesome.

So, it can be implied; it doesn't have to be done absolutely obviously in the way that it's done in traditional music. There are various subtle ways by which one can imply this eternal presence without actually just sounding the note all the time. You can remove it to indicate the apparent absence of the divine presence, or you can transfer *its* presence into the proliferation of choral and orchestral writing, implying that the divine presence has become 'at one' with everything.

Music comes out of silence and falls back into silence – music is only living while it's sounded. So this single note is the articulation of the eternal silence, the nearest you can get to the very root of music in the world of articulated sound? The ison announces the possibility of the whole sound world that subsequently follows?
Yes. And usually it will start the piece of music, as it does in all traditional chanting, and usually will end it. It comes out of silence with no real beginning and no real end, so in a sense it is never not present. But it's a very different silence from the silence that I hear in Webern, for instance, because, as we agreed earlier, his silence is an abstract silence, not a sacred silence.

I recall at the rehearsals and at the first performance of Mary of Egypt, *where you asked the eternity note to begin gradually and to become audible very slowly, I recall thinking this was a very evocative way of drawing the whole sound world of the piece out of the eternal silence.*
As it is representing eternity, it doesn't need to be too dominant. If you go to an Orthodox liturgy on Mount Athos you'll find that the *ison* is very strong. But I don't want to copy traditional music

in such a direct way, only convey the ethos of it. It isn't a *sine qua non* for every single piece I write, however. That would be far too horribly logical, and the mystery would lose its potency.

Since in a metaphysical context it might be said that nothing is insignificant, what might be the occasions when the absence of the drone has a particular significance?
As I hinted before, when the *ison* has been present and suddenly it's taken away, that has a dramatic significance, maybe of 'Divine Darkness' or the apparent 'absence' of God. Also, there are certain pieces where I just don't want the eternity note, although it might be present, to use Western terminology, as a kind of pedal point.

If you think of the marvellously grave opening five bars of Bach's *St Matthew Passion*, one could say the eternity note was present there. It never moves off the pedal E, and it always disappoints me when Bach starts climbing up the scale with the succeeding bars. Then, for me, that sense of the eternal ebbs away.

Handel does a similarly wonderful thing for evoking pastoral situations, by just holding a continuous pedal point – that's what he would have called it because that would be the Western term.

Are there other ways of establishing the eternal in your music?
If one uses the harmony of the spheres, or if one uses scales connected with the cosmos, which comes from Pythagoras or Plato or various musicians through the ages. But we are living in an age that does not believe that sound is capable of putting us in touch with higher levels of reality. So I am out on a limb. In a piece like *Agraphon*, for instance, I use the harmonic series, and that's a series of endlessly spiralling intervals that have a divine significance. Stockhausen does it in *Stimmung*, by using music of the spheres in that single chord – and all power to both our elbows.

Coming back to the idea that in a metaphysical context nothing is without significance, what is the significance of silence itself in your music?

There's a literal use of silence, which I use in a number of pieces – I think particularly of *The Apocalypse* and *Resurrection* – even in some of the small choral pieces. Everything I write, in fact, has literal silence. The music just stops. I usually specify for how many seconds the silence should last.

Then there is another kind of silence, which I connect to ikons. If you look at the very great ikons of the Byzantine period, you see angels transfixed as they gaze upon God. I've often thought: is it possible to produce that kind of ecstatic frozen petrified silence in music? I've certainly tried to do it in various pieces. This kind of silence one could almost take even further and say it was frozen or uncreated Eros, because it comes in the form of longing (this is something beyond the yearning of religious sentiment), it's a petrified longing, it's a longing that goes beyond the longing of one person for another. Or perhaps it doesn't: it's not my business to qualify that. Anyway, it is the longing for God. Maybe you can see God in another person – you should be able to see God in all people – but it's that longing. I'm particularly aware of it during the Holy Week services. 'I see your bridal chamber adorned, O my saviour, yet I have no fitting garment to enter therein: but do thou shine, shine on the robe of my soul.' This longing for God which, as in ikons, is somehow petrified and silent.

Is there ever a silence for you that is simply the absence of sound?

I don't think so, because when heard correctly I would say that even when music is sounding there is, or there should be, an implicit silence – certainly in my music. If there is no implicit silence, somehow the music is not doing what I want it to do.

There's another kind of silence which one hears in the music of Webern. I would say this is certainly a qualitative silence, as we have agreed, but it's an ascetic, scholastic silence. Webern was a complex composer who was carrying on up to a point the

German tradition of development, progress and all the rest of it. Therefore it can only be an abstract silence.

It's akin to what one might call an idealized geometry.
Yes, and not like a frozen ecstasy, which is a much more Platonic concept of silence. Webern was a Roman Catholic and a scholastic, and his music is, as Stravinsky said, analytical. When I listen to his music I always sense what is beyond the notes. His silence seems to acknowledge another dimension so that there is a wonderful transparency in his music which somehow allows God to enter – it's not clogged up, as so much Western music is. Webern's music is not just modern, it doesn't belong just to the twentieth century.

Webern and late Stravinsky stand quite alone in this respect. They both transcend the standard Western music which excludes by an over-proliferation of notes and therefore excludes God himself. In such late pieces as *Threni*, *Canticum Sacrum*, *Abraham and Isaac*, the *Variations* (in memory of Aldous Huxley) and even in a piece like *Agon*, Stravinsky achieved a marvellous transparency.

Of course we don't know what is the silence of eternity as such: eternity seen from God's point of view, if you like.

When I came upon the section in *The Apocalypse* where St John speaks of there being no more heaven and no more earth, no more moon, no more sun, because everything is one, when I first tried to set this, I had the idea that maybe there should be a totally resounding triumphal way of expressing it. But then I realized I was dealing with something that was inexpressible and I had to go about it in the manner of a *via negativa* – I had to strip the music bare. So what happens in this section – the New Jerusalem, about which we know nothing – I just have a single note pulsing on all the instruments, all the voices, intensely quietly. It's a canon in many, many parts on a single note.

Could it be said that your music points to silence as the ultimate auditory state?

I have met certain Orthodox monks – in their presence you feel that the saints of old continue to live amongst us, because, like them, they are 'dead to the world'. 'Dead to the world' translates for me in auditory terms as 'silent music'.

Let's turn now to performances and performers. Because so much of what you intend in your music, especially in your more recent works, and what you require of your performers, is so different from what Western performers are trained to give and respond to, I'm prompted to ask to what extent your music needs a different tradition of performance and performers?
At this point I am not going to answer the question, because it can only be answered properly in a true meeting of minds. I'll quote C. S. Lewis (and suggest that any performer of my music should first of all read this), and then see how I can be more specific, but also try to show how the ethos helps the technique.

> In the darkness something was happening at last. A voice had begun to sing. It was very far away and Digory found it hard to decide from what direction it was coming. Sometimes it seemed to come from all directions at once. Sometimes he almost thought it was coming out of the earth beneath them. Its lower notes were deep enough to be the voice of the earth herself. There were no words. There was hardly even a tune . . . You would have felt quite certain that it was the stars themselves who were singing, and that it was the First Voice, the deep one, which had made them appear, made them sing . . .

This clearly refers to the Christ figure, the created logos by whom all things are made. In a sense my music has nothing to do with me – if it is anything at all it is like the song which C. S. Lewis describes. If the performers understand his song, they will understand my music.
Clearly Gennady Rozhdestvensky fits into all this, particularly with the *Akhmatova Requiem*. I knew it from the start, immediately I heard the first bars. He made me amazed by my own

music. After the first performance in the Usher Hall in Edinburgh, he came up to me and did something to me that showed more than just an affinity and a great affection. He made the Orthodox sign of the Cross over me. It denotes a degree of connection between us that is beyond this transient world.

More recently, you've felt there was a special affinity between a young Greek conductor and some performances of your music. Yes, Alexandros Mirat. He's the conductor of the Camerata Orchestra at the Megaron in Athens. I've never come across a conductor who introduced a new piece in quite the way he introduced *Agraphon*. He said to the young players, 'You must play it as if these are the last notes you will ever play. You must play it at the absolute limit of intensity.' Then he did another thing which impressed me very much, but maybe that's because he was trained by Celibidache, he tuned each individual section of the strings on their own, so the pitch was like a string quartet or a small group of instruments.

Alexandros conducts *Agraphon* in a way that I've never heard anybody else conduct it. They are all young players in the Camerata; they are from Greece, Russia, Scotland and other countries. They play with a white heat of intensity that makes you sit on the edge of your seat. They want to know what the piece is all about – even the symbolism of it. Alexandros is a brilliant musician who has an understanding that goes beyond understanding. His players don't simply play the notes, they play also what is *behind* the notes and hence they are able to make the audience 'cry'.

There is also the main cellist in the Camerata, who plays *The Protecting Veil* – I can't say he plays it better, all I can say is that he played it in a way that was more authentic than anyone else; I mean more authentic in the sense that his instrument no longer sounded like a cello, which I suppose was my original intention. It sounded hardly human, more like the voice of the Mother of God.

Of course, Steven Isserlis's performance is absolutely wonderful. He has played *The Protecting Veil* all over the world. He told me that when he performed it in Japan, he saw many young girls cry. I don't know whether that's just a Japanese habit or a reaction to my music. Good or bad. Even when he's playing my quartets, Steven always wants to know the meaning behind the notes. But he is exceptional.

You mentioned earlier that you have recently become associated with the Academy of Ancient Music, and you're hoping this might be a fruitful collaboration in the future.
I was immensely impressed by the kind of musicians they were, the fact that they took an interest in the meaning of the piece – beyond the notes, that is. They wanted to know all that. And Paul Goodwin, their conductor, seemed able to identify at a very deep level with the music.

As to who else has been associated with my music almost throughout my composing career, the one who comes immediately to mind is Martin Neary, who's performed almost every piece of my music, and his understanding of it is deeply intuitive. Likewise Richard Hickox. I am very lucky to have this kind of commitment. With Levon Chilingirian, with his Armenian Orthodox background, I have the perfect quartet to perform my three quartets. My relationship with the Tallis Scholars and Peter Phillips is also special: I'm the only living composer that the Tallis Scholars have commissioned.

I must say, however, that Gennadi and Alexandros have an esoteric connection with my music, both by their own common spirituality and the kind of people they are. For instance, I am not used to standing next to one of my performers waiting for Holy Unction during Holy Week in the Orthodox Church: but, behold, there was Gennady! Neither am I used to talking to my performers about the relationship between Zen and Orthodoxy – as I did with Alexandros. Now this is what I mean by 'ethos' having an overwhelming effect on technique, and therefore on the high quality of performance.

Of course, I hope I am not so myopic as to say that all my performers must be Orthodox. But they must have a connection to the music that is other than the notes. They must be open, like the young players in the Athens Camerata, the Gogmagogs, the BT Ensemble with Clio Gould, and the Academy of Ancient Music with Paul Goodwin. I say two words like 'more Eastern' and they produce the perfect result.

Let's look now to the future, and the way in which your music questions the whole apparatus of Western music-making. As a pointer in that direction, I think of the one person you've written most works for, and who seems to, as it were, set a standard of interpretation in a way that no other performer has, and that's of course Patricia Rozario. As well as being Indian and Catholic and being trained in the West, Patricia has a very rare, even unique ability in her voice, one might even say in her blood, to interpret your work.
Absolutely so. One might almost say that when she sings my music she actually becomes it. This is something incredibly rare and, most of all, is to do with the fact that she is Indian. Her technique opens out when she sings my music: she does things she never thought she could do, not because she has technique – plenty of other singers have that – but because she believes the music. Yes, that is exactly the term: she believes it. She can identify with my music totally and she goes right to the core of it. There's a complete lack of the cerebral in her voice, which is why I think she does not sing Western music with the depth of communication she brings to my music, which has a mixture of Eastern and Western elements in it.

Can I push you to be a little more specific about this quality of her voice?
It's not the voice as such. It's what happens to it when her voice 'touches' my music. I remember when she came to my house and sang Mozart. I had no reaction. Then I said, 'Sing these notes' – something from *Mary of Egypt* – and at once she went out of herself, and started to become Mary of Egypt. Patricia is able somehow to transcend the artifices of Western music. If I said to

her, 'You transcend the artifices of Western music', she would collapse with laughter. But she has the ability to express uncreated ecstasy and a tenderness that is almost beyond earthly sentiment. Also, the Indian quality of her voice enables her to sound primordial while at the same time she has the range of a frivolous coloratura in the West. Her voice sounds primordial at the bottom end and ecstatic (not frivolous) at the top. She can sustain a spiritual intensity which I've not come across in any other singer. She can also become totally possessed by the music, especially in *Agraphon*. And in the soft singing she has the ability to articulate ecstatic silence.

That is what I need from every performer. I have to insist, any future performers of my music must understand what lies beyond the notes. Otherwise the music will not exist at all. We're always going back to metaphysics – as I've said, I consider my music is liquid metaphysics. I clearly cannot demand belief in what I believe in, but I can ask for an openness, or certainly an acceptance that another level of reality exists beyond this commonplace one.

One could send certain performers off to Psalti or Indian masters and they would come back in exactly the same condition as they were before they went – even if they had the most amazing voices in the world. I have said young performers are pliable and can react very quickly, with just a mere suggestion. But a singer or performer who has been used to just singing or playing Mozart, Brahms and Boulez will never be able to sing or play my music. It would be like asking Owen Brannigan to sing *The Last Discourse*.

If performers or conductors really *want* to perform my music then that is the first thing. It will mean they have begun to understand that there is something behind the notes. Then, if they want to take it further, they will investigate, either practically by going to a master, or, hopefully, intuitively realizing that what is *not* present in the score – the printed notes – is far more important.

Six Commentaries

Mary of Egypt

Without the collaboration of Mother Thekla, *Mary of Egypt* could never have been written. I wanted to know the theology of the desert in all its searing compassion, but I also wanted an almost childlike text, not unlike early Coptic ikons. *Mary of Egypt* stands or falls by the recognition of the shock of its simplicity, both in the music and in the text. The music reflects the simplicity in the incredibly tight use of the material.

The subject of *Mary of Egypt* had long haunted me – the story of an early Christian harlot saint and the meeting with a holy man in the desert. How could one call the whore, Mary of Egypt, good, even though she never took money for her prostitution? How could one question the holy man Zossima at all? Precisely because Mary's door was wide open, even though her love was misdirected and distorted. As Zossima's door was closing around him, with his pride, even though he understood all mysteries, even though he was a recognized holy man, even though he could perform miracles, he had not found the one thing needful, the supreme mystery of the humility essential for love.

We see the two figures, ikon-like, in parallel lines: Mary whoring without singing words in Alexandria, so in the first part of the piece she only makes the noise 'Ah' – there are no words. Zossima is extremely verbose and rather stuck in his world of so-called holiness, with the help of a small group of singing and acting women and men representing the extensions of Mary and Zossima respectively. Then there was the Voice, unseen and unembodied. The voice I had in mind was that of a Middle East-

ern singer, or an Indian singer who had a knowledge of microtones, but was also able to read Western notation. It took me a
long time to find such a voice but finally I found it in Chloe
Goodchild, who early in life had been trained in Western music
and now was devoting her life to singing music of the East. She
was able to sing this disembodied voice.

Mary is led into the desert after travelling to Jerusalem, not as
a pilgrim but because that way she could see a lot of men on
board ship and she wanted to direct her love towards them.
Eventually, finding herself at the doors of the Church of the Holy
Sepulchre in Jerusalem, and not because God prevents her, but
because of something inside herself, she is prevented from going
in. She makes three attempts to go into the church and finally she
allows herself to go in – I think I must put it that way – something within her allows her to enter. She finds herself underneath
the ikon of the Mother of God who seems to be saying to her that
she must go into the desert, where she will then live for forty
years. Under the scorched sun and freezing winters of the desert
her skin becomes very blackened and she loses her clothes.

After many years have elapsed and after a period in a
monastery near the desert, Zossima finds what he has been
searching for. Quoting from the libretto: 'Perfection, once an
abstract sound of grace, takes form in you, most gracious of
your kind.' Zossima's whole sound world, which has up till now
been very masculine, joins Mary's sound world, which is feminine. In her he sees love and his own limitations. His world, once
so dry, now in the dryness of the desert flowers into what the
desert fathers might have called 'uncreated Eros', or a hint of the
Edenic state. In controlled ecstasy they both ask each other to
give the blessing and they prostrate in front of each other – as it
says in the hagiography – for what seems to be an eternity. Mary
then levitates as the angels lift her up. Zossima is, to begin with,
terrified and awestruck and cannot leave her: 'If only I may just
look on you for ever.' He is an old man who has, in one sense,
fallen in love with Mary because he wants to look at her; he asks
her, 'I don't want to gaze upon anybody else, only to gaze on

you.' But she is quite stern and tells him no, he must return to his monastery, then come back to her the following year, to give her what she most desires: the body and blood of Christ.

A year later and in a series of mimed inserts, Zossima mimes his grief as he comes once more to look for her. He sees her over the other side of a river, and in despair thinks, I cannot cross, there is no boat. How can I see her? How can she cross to me? But she walks over the water – as Christ walked on the Sea of Galilee – receives communion and tells the desolate Zossima to go away and return again the following year. She returns, walking on the water.

A year elapses and Zossima comes again. This time he cannot find her anywhere. Suddenly he sees her lying dead in the sand with an instruction marked into it, 'Bury humble Mary'. Redeemed nature appears in the form of a lion, tame in the presence of the remains of the saint, and helps feeble Zossima to bury humble Mary with his busy paws.

Mary of Egypt is an attempt to create an ikon in sound about non-judgement: we know and yet we do not know; the double ignorance; the Pharisee and the Publican and the Prodigal Son; the woman taken in adultery: judge not, judge not, judge not. The whole piece is loosely based on the ancient Byzantine hymn '*Tin Oreotita*' ('Awed by thy beauty'), sung to the Mother of God. In a sense Zossima loves again when through Mary he can see the beauty of God. Who knows how far Mary has gone in her search of the unknowable and unattainable in her forty solitary years in the desert?

Mary of Egypt now seems to me to be one of the most feminine works that I have ever written, both in its sound – the sound of its flutes, again much influenced by the *nāy* (I instruct the flutes to be played in the authentic Middle Eastern style), and in its subject, which is deeply feminine. It was as if Zossima had to enter Mary's feminine, spiritual 'sound world' before he could understand divine love. He is truly awed by her beauty. Perhaps the whole piece is an example of uncreated Eros.

The origin of the piece goes back to my reading a book by Mother Thekla. She prints the hagiography of the actual story and then she comments on it. I was very impressed by the way that she did not dismiss the first part of Mary's life. I'd known about this story for a long time; it haunted me. But what had always put me off using it was a certain Father's insistence that the only important part about Mary of Egypt is the second part of her life; the first part was nothing. What impressed me about Mother Thekla's account was the way she was able to connect the two and say that literally the one could not exist without the other. They were, in fact, different sides of the same coin. It haunted me, so much so that I dreamt about this figure running away from Zossima in the desert. This vivid memory, I have to say, was never realized in the production that I saw of it.

I suppose I also thought, however vaguely, that this theme had something to say to our times, because of the appalling narrowness of the concept of the erotic. The erotic for me is present in all the Orthodox services in Holy Week. It is present every time I start writing. We narrow it to such an appalling degree, to just the biological sexual act, whereas it is really part of everything. Look out of the window, look at a tree, indeed music or any of the arts – all these things have a connection with Eros. I certainly did not write *Mary of Egypt* in order to make a sermon on Eros, but in order to explore the spiritual connection between man and woman.

The musical material of *Mary of Egypt* is very tightly controlled. Certain music is given to Mary and certain music and rhythms are given to Zossima. Every time they appear, Mary is accompanied by a flute, and Zossima by trombone and simantron. (The simantron is an ancient Byzantine instrument made of wood or metal; it is beaten with a mallet to the rhythm 'O *tâla ton*, O *tâla ton*, O *tâla tâla tâla ton*, reminding the monks that they must use their talents.) The nearer he gets to Mary, so his sound world starts to become integrated with Mary's sound world. In the first part the rhythm of the simantron is turned upside-down, and when she is doing her whoring the rhythms of the simantron are used to actually depict the opposite of a high spiritual state. The simantron itself is not used but drums and voices are used when she sings. Sometimes she sings in the rhythm of the simantron.

There is nothing erotic whatsoever in the sound of a simantron being played in a monastery to call the monks to prayer. And there is nothing erotic whatsoever in the music of Zossima, who again uses this rhythm, but in a very dry way. Not only is the whole work based on this fragment of Byzantine chant – 'Awed by thy beauty' – but also that is what Zossima actually is: he is awed by the beauty of Mary of Egypt, both the inner and the outer beauty. There is nothing really in *Mary of Egypt* which is not interconnected.

In so far as I call *Mary of Egypt* a moving ikon, nothing in it should be naturalistic. Every single movement should be choreographed exactly, austerely; with each movement certain themes and rhythms should be heard by way of identity. I am almost saying: serialize the movement, so that every movement, every gesture of the hand – rather like in Indian dancing or Noh drama – actually corresponds to something heard in the music. This was not done at its Aldeburgh production, which was for me a matter of regret. I think the piece would have come much more alive if we had worked out a system of symbolic gestures: whenever the simantron sounds, there should be a corresponding movement; whenever Mary's flute music sounds, there should be some sort of gesture. So, depending on whatever spiritual state, or state of sensuality, is appropriate to the action, one would recognize it in the music just as one recognized Mary with the flutes and Zossima with the simantron and trombone.

Just as there is no scope for the performers in this piece to, as it were, improvise on a spontaneous basis, so also the audience must come to see the piece in the expectation of making some effort to accommodate its somewhat hieratic formality. Philip Sherrard had said many years before that it should be a liturgy of Eros. That is what it finally is. In a sense the audience comes to a liturgical event. They are not coming to an opera. The whole thing is a symbol. It is not 'realistic'. Ideally it should be performed with masks, so the audience and the action, such as it is, are removed from the sphere of the personal.

I should add that there are *no* musical models for *Mary of Egypt*.

The Toll Houses

When I read a book by a Californian monk, Father Seraphim Rose, called *The Toll Houses*, I was greatly intrigued. The concept of the Toll Houses is not exactly a dogma of the Orthodox Church. The idea that the soul passes through aerial Toll Houses during a number of days after death, I found very interesting both as a spiritual thing and particularly as a musical idea. There is an almost comic ikon of the Toll Houses, with some people falling down off a ladder into the flames and others being able to get higher and higher and going through the Toll Houses. The whole concept is a kind of first judgement, not the Last Judgement – an under-heaven judgement of people when they die. They go through twenty-three different Toll Houses.

The Toll Houses in themselves are the posthumous states of being of the soul, where it is decided whether the soul spends a certain period of time in hell and a certain period of time in heaven. But one has to understand this is all symbolical. This theme whetted my appetite musically because it suggested ritual, it suggested symbol, in fact it suggested many different things.

When I sent the book to Mother Thekla she was totally outraged by the idea that anybody could have any idea at all about what happens after death. Nevertheless, in due course she sent me a text that left me absolutely flabbergasted. I didn't know what to do with it. All the seriousness, all the ritual had been taken out and it read like a parody of the Toll Houses – like a Whitehall farce. But eventually *The Toll Houses* was completed and the following is offered as a philosophical and theological note on it.

I, the real I, is this other, this mostly submerged and unheeded source of my being. There is, of course, a difference in man between his innermost self and the self with which he usually and mistakenly identifies himself, his everyday self. It is this double nature of his being, the fact of his possessing a more superficial empirical self that is capable of ignoring and even of becoming impervious to his inner self, that is the most evident symptom of that internal dislocation of man's being. In the Orthodox Christian tradition this is indicated by the term 'fall'.

Man, then, is double in himself: there is a Cain and there is an Abel, and indeed the Cain in him – his superficial ego – is ever capable of denying and so metaphysically killing the real source of his being, his own inner depth, the Abel in him. In so far as he acts at the behest of the Cain within himself, so he is truly in the power of the enemy, the evil one, Satan. However, what man is in his inmost self, that which determines and qualifies all aspects of his existence, is neither temporal nor relative but eternal and absolute. Man himself may be totally unaware of this grace inherent in him: again and again in our age this appears to be the norm, but it *is* present in him, whether he is aware of it or not.

According to Orthodox legend or tradition, at death the soul is subjected to a series of tests at fixed stations or Toll Houses. Subject to its performance at these tests, the soul is directed to heaven or to hell, where it will await the Last Judgement. The tests, in effect, are related in my piece not to the twenty-three stations or Toll Houses, but to the seven mortal sins. (This was the idea of Mother Thekla, the librettist.) The purpose of the Toll Houses is to suggest that we cannot know the divine judgement on any soul. Thus we see a character, Beatrice, apparently failing at every test, yet by the end no judgement has been pronounced nor even suggested. The action begins for the second time in the precise manner of the first, to reiterate the fact that the human mind can never reach a solution or a conclusion but must ever begin again. Each Toll House represents, in my version of it, the enacting of one of the deadly or mortal sins: pride, covetousness, lust, envy, gluttony, anger, sloth. Throughout the music there is a parallel of action: Beatrice is dead and her soul is being tested. Thus we have the unseen singing voice of the soul, at once in torment, tender, lyrical and ecstatic, accompanying the mundane living corpse, at once frivolous and butterfly-minded.

Beatrice's 'friends' who accompany her on her journey are both women and at the same time they are singing angels: one, a guardian angel, and the other, a fallen angel. Beatrice enjoys a pleasant outing. She does not realize that she is dead. She thinks that she has had a long illness and that she's going on an outing to the zoo. When she gets to this aerial zoo she encounters different animals, animals that she would have known from her childhood visits to the zoo. However, what the good angel wants her to see are not these animals but a series of boring, sinful human beings. She only sees amusing animals. The sin in her and the subjective nature of her vision are emphasized by the duplication of her features throughout the tests. The singing voice of her soul is always at odds with the frivolous speaking self. The dichotomy between the speaking Beatrice and her singing soul is therefore the crux of the whole piece – the impossibility of human judgement, either in life or death. At each Toll House her apparent failure in succumbing to the charm of sin seems obvious, but at the end of each test she comes down, not as yet to hell, but to rejoin her earthly corpse which is actually in a coffin. She's not alone in this testing process. Other souls, apparently visitors at the zoo, are being dragged down into the flaming furnaces of hell, or making some steps up the ladder towards heaven. Only at the end, as the Devil prepares to claim his own, there comes a shock: no answer. Has she failed? We do not know.

The key point for the producer is the passage of Beatrice's soul. Once this is understood metaphysically and musically, a visual counterpoint must be found for it and then the rest, with all its contradictions, should become clear. The existing libretto should only be used as a guideline. However, it is essential that whoever produces it has steeped him- or herself in tradition and in the symbolism and the metaphysics of the Eastern Church. Beyond that, we must use as much imagination and ingenuity as possible.

The music of *The Toll Houses* is in one sense the boldest undertaking that I have made, in so far as I have used, within tradition, irony. The symbols, the metaphors, the musical metaphysics apply to every note of this work something like a secret language. The music of Beatrice's soul, for instance, acts as a guideline or musical graph, to tell the listener where the state of her soul is at any given point in the metaphysical pantomime. The music of the symbolism relates to the Bridegroom services of Holy Week in the Orthodox Church: 'Behold the Bridegroom comes at midnight – beware lest you find yourself sleeping.' The music is contorted, inverted, perverted, transfigured. Every group of instruments has a symbolic function. For instance, the strings, just violins and double basses – no violas, no cellos – often tell us of the spiritual state. The trombones represent the lions. The jazz trumpets represent the fornicating monkeys.

As to its performance, ideally it has to be simple and should take place in a large building that is not necessarily an opera house and preferably in the round. The Albert Hall is a possibility. In fact there is a strong possibility that it may be staged in the Albert Hall at one of the Proms in 2001. That would be ideal.

Also, I'm in touch with a Russian film producer who worked with Tarkovsky. Andrei Konchalovsky envisages using a Russian family of clowns, three of them, so that they can by different masks and different gestures suggest animals and at the same time pompous businessmen who sing litanies about making money, making money, more and more and more and more. So it would be done by a small group of people, not by a huge cast – by these clowns who Andrei says are the most brilliant that he's ever seen. They can do absolutely anything.

In a way I envisage the trombones at least standing up when they are lions, the jazz trumpets at least standing up when they are monkeys. I think it can be quite vulgar, quite Hollywoody in places. For instance, I can envisage the clowns pulling faces, although frozen at certain points when the heavenly choirs are singing 'Behold the Bridegroom comes at midnight'. And some of them can stick their tongues out at this. At all events it must be really crazy, and as Mother Thekla says, '*dangerous* on all levels'.

The form of *The Toll Houses* is very rigorous indeed, and it is reminiscent of the structure of Orthodox services. I should say that during the composition of *The Toll Houses* I read extensively books on tradition, from Guénon and Coomaraswamy to Frithjof Schuon, and I am eternally grateful to them.

The Toll Houses will succeed or fail by its ability to communicate on different levels by the language of pantomime, by the language of metaphysics or, you could say, the language of circus and the language of metaphysics. If it succeeds, it will be understood on one level by a six-year-old and I hope on another level by a sixty-year-old.

Short Choral Works

It has always seemed to me that music should serve the community, in so far as there is any community left in this new age of barbarism. I regard my shorter choral pieces, which must number over one hundred at least, as a traditional craft and at the same time a way of serving what is left of our community. Pieces such as *The Lamb* (1982), *Song for Athene* (1993), *As One Who Has Slept* (1996), *Two Hymns to the Mother of God* (1985), *The Annunciation* (1992) – these are performed all over the world, from India to Peru. These short pieces can be sung by cathedral choirs or amateur choirs everywhere, and although it is the Orthodox Church which has inspired them, the Western Church sings them. It is for me humbling and at the same time a great honour, to give what I am able to the Western Church, having drunk deeply from the eternal depths of the one true Orthodox Church.

All composers should, I think, be able to write simple music that can be sung by amateur forces. This for me is a kind of litmus test of the art of the true composer and the true traditionalist. It is to tradition alone that I aspire in everything that I try to do. How close I come to it is not for me, or indeed anyone else, to judge.

When I say these pieces are examples of traditional craft, I have in mind that they can serve what is left of the community and in a way that functions on different levels. For instance, there are certain people who look at ikons or they look at stained-glass windows and they can just see it as a kind of fable from the Bible, or they may see it on a much deeper level. That is what these short choral pieces should be. If I am asked to write a carol for King's College, Cambridge, for instance, I hope I would not write a sentimental sweet piece of rubbish with no metaphysical meaning whatsoever and no comprehension of the incarnation.

Whenever I have set existing texts they have come either from Blake or from Yeats or from the Orthodox Christmas Vigil or from ancient medieval texts. Many years ago, carols were not sung before Christmas, only sung after; before was considered as a period of preparation for Christmas, a period of fasting, certainly in the Eastern Church. In the Western Church it was the period of Advent and was seen very much like the period of Lent before Easter.

If I am asked to write a carol I feel I should be able to do it within a couple of hours. It is something that should and normally does come to me very quickly. Think of somebody like Bach writing a cantata for every day of the Protestant Church's calendar. He is a supreme example of a traditional craftsman of the highest order. Technically everybody should aspire to what Bach does with the chorale. Every chorale of Bach is magical, and the tune is often not his own, but what he does with it is quite wonderful. Technically, I suppose, I do the same thing, sometimes perhaps using a Byzantine melody or using a snippet of Russian medieval chant.

Also, because I am writing it for the 'other', I am not writing it really for myself, so I hope there will be no indulgence in it. I see these choral pieces as exercises in self-effacement.

The Apocalypse

The Apocalypse is such a great mystery that I do not want to write at length about it, and I also feel that, more than with any other work of mine, reaction to it depends on the spiritual sensitivity of each individual listener.

'We all await and stand in need of the presence of those who come out of the great tribulation over whom death no longer has power'. Out of his burning, thundering love, St John sees the vision of the end – beyond all comprehension, imagination and thought. A giant apocalyptic proliferation of the single note D with which *The Apocalypse* begins and ends: everything else dances in and out of this eternity note.

The spatial disposition of the musical forces represents symbolically their spiritual significance. At the highest level the Voice of God, and then the woman clothed with the sun plus the trumpets, trombones, timpani and tam-tams. On the intermediate level, the counter-tenors and recorders, representing the angels. On the ground level the violins, the double basses and Seven Church choirs of the Apocalypse. And finally the Whore of Babylon, who makes a dramatic appearance signifying the 'mirror' image of the woman clothed with the sun.

	Prologue
ICON I	The Seven Churches on earth
ICON II	Heaven (Adoration of The Messiah *before* the last events)
ICON III	Six Seals (Vision of events *before* Day of Judgement)
ICON IV	Seventh Seal (Six trumpets – visions of six events of destruction *before* Day of Judgement)
ICON V	Seventh Trumpet: six visions (The Messiah – His 'History')

ICON VI   Seventh Vision: six vials (Visions of six events of
           actual destruction before the Day of Judgement)
ICON VII   Seventh Vial: six visions (Visions of six events
           IN FACT *before* the Day of Judgement)
ICON VIII Seventh Vision: Last Judgement (Heaven –
           Judgement *after* last events)
ICON IX   The New Jerusalem (Beyond everything).

This might give some idea of the scale and the divinely linked nature of this massive piece. I try, by using immense spatial dimensions, the organically interrelated material, the variants, the perversions, as well as the outbursts of splendour, to show something of the awe and the terror and the abundant love that thunders down on us. In the New Jerusalem section, since it is beyond *everything*, I abandon music for metaphysics and allow the note of eternity to pulse around the building in a giant canon on the note D, worked out with mathematical precision sung and played as quietly as possible. A marriage of mathematics and metaphysics.

One facetious critic had the inanity (and in this case the *heresy*) to call this work 'Air on a D String'. If that is all a member of the human race can find to say about this colossal warning in musical metaphysics, I fear that we are living in the Last Days. As St John turns his tender plea to Christ at the end, 'Come Lord, come quickly', I cannot help thinking that provided the world still exists, one day *The Apocalypse* will perhaps be seen to be the most 'necessary' music for the turn of the century.

Fall and Resurrection

I wanted to write something about Paradise – the original Edenic state – and the Fall. That was the first idea. The second idea was brought about by discussions with Prince Charles. He remarked what a wonderful idea it might be if I wrote something that dealt with music connected with before time and right up to the Resurrection. I had to find a way of expressing this vast subject – the vastest subject I have ever tackled.

I asked Mother Thekla whether she thought this was possible and she went silent, as she often does, for about two weeks. Then I received through the post a very terse libretto which was just full of hints: sounds of the prophets, sounds of the incarnation – maybe single words, almost Beckett-like in its constraint. As she has often said in recent collaborations, 'I really only want to give you a few words, hints, for you to find the music.'

In its three-part structure, *Fall and Resurrection* tries to encompass by means of these terse hints what has taken place since the beginning of time and even before time. The whole of creation is not a random process without meaning and purpose. On the other hand, man is not bound to his historical destiny as if he were a convict in a chain-gang, without choice or freedom.

With these presuppositions in place, I felt I had to begin in God's Paradise, not our Paradise, but God in Paradise. It is beyond me to know what that is, so the work begins in total silence. The lights of the building should fade and there will be a conducted sixty seconds of silence. Then we begin to hear a series of very slow, at this stage apparently unrelated notes. Gradually these notes become an almost inaudible chord on the strings. Then starts some of the most complicated music that I've ever written.

I had to ask myself, how on earth do I represent uncreated chaos – what does this mean, what is uncreated chaos? Is God present? Presumably God *must* be present. What does chaos mean in musical terms? For me, it just is ante-primordial chaos. But since God must have been present in this very difficult to imagine uncreated chaos, what I decided to do was to take from a Byzantine chant, '*Ton stavrón sou*' – 'Thy cross O Christ we adore' – a matrix of notes, and to give it forty permutations, all being played on different instruments, with about twenty-seven different tempi. All this with some instruments moving at, say, crotchet equals 30, all the way up to something like crotchet equals 280, and moving almost beyond audibility because it goes, as it were, beyond the sound barrier.

I remember reading something of St Dionysios the Areopagite at this particular point: 'All things remain still and move at dizzying speed towards some end without end, which is itself a beginning without beginning . . .'

I might say, by the way, that the construction of it was a huge mathematical undertaking for me. It took me a month to compose each page, and because the complexity of the variants was so great, I had to redo the pages sometimes twice, sometimes three times. If you heard this music out of context, you might think that you were listening to a piece of the 'new complexity', except there is an underlying sound which never goes away.

As the music of this vastly complicated beginning proceeds, this underlying sound becomes stronger as the chaos becomes greater. They crescendo with each other until, dramatically, the conductor makes a sign, and the chaos suddenly stops. Then emerges this constant sound which has been there all the way through the chaos, a bottom G on the double basses – the presence of God.

In this chaos all the potentials of good and evil are heard – and that again was a very important metaphysical point I had to consider in musical construction. Out of this chaos, God, who has been forever present during this chaos, loves the world into being: the world, an earthly paradise, a monody without confusion. This is played on the *nāy* (the work is going to be performed in St Paul's), which will sound from high up at the west end of the cathedral and which should sound prelapsarian in its innocence. I always connect the sound of the *nāy* with prelapsarian innocence. (At St Paul's we will use the *kaval* because it has greater range.)

Then one hears the voice of Adam, and after a while the voice of Eve. They sing openly and primordially, to each other and to God. Some false notes start to appear. For example, in the terse manner of the libretto, Adam sings the one word 'apple', which Eve takes up also. Then, at a certain cosmic moment, the word 'apple tree' is sung both by Adam and by Eve. At this point there is a terrifying sound from the orchestra, not related to the uncreated chaos theme, and at a remote distance from the orchestra (from the Whispering Gallery) a ram's-horn trumpet is heard playing the traditional rhythms of that primordial instrument. The music starts to dislocate and the simple monody is destroyed. Seen musically, one could say that for the first time there is a musical 'fall' taking place, because of the introduction of musical formulae, counterpoint, complexity, drama, sensuality and dissonance – and man-made techniques.

The next word one hears is the word 'knowledge' and the chaos increases. It climaxes when everybody – the choir, Adam and Eve – sing, 'We are God.' There are more blasts from the ram's-horn trumpet, and fear is introduced. So emotion is present in the music for the first time, whereas before there was none at all. Sadness appears. The Devil appears. These introductions are both instrumental and vocal. You hear the word 'fallen', 'fallen', 'fallen', many times, 'cast out', 'cast out from Paradise', Adam weeping outside Paradise with Eve, 'no scent', 'no breeze', 'no innocence', 'no scent', 'no breeze', 'no innocence', 'fallen', 'gates locked against ourselves', 'out'. Now the notion of work appears – Paradise lost. And then you hear the deeply tragic and solemn voice of God sounding from the very highest point (in the dome): 'I planted you a precious vine of pure and noble stock; how did you become a vine degenerate?' That is the beginning of the first of the work's three parts.

Patristic theology tells us of the divine original state representing a series of theophanies, and even in its fallen state it is seen to present forms whose contemplation may lead the mind back to an awareness of divine beauty.

The link between the first and the second part is the link between the Fall and the Incarnation. This link is the prophets, because they saw in the darkness. In this section of the work, verses or hints from the prophets and the psalmist – the divine David – are sung by a counter-tenor. The Fall was once and for all, but we have the choice. We have the choice because of the Incarnation of the Logos.

The second part also begins with complex and contrapuntal music until one hears, again, the *nāy* (or the *kaval*), but no longer undecorated. There is the sound of dissonance underneath it. But there are the divine links, the prophets, words from the Psalms, words from prophets of the Old Testament, sung by a counter-tenor, 'up to a land of milk and honey . . .'. Then the very quiet, awesome sound, 'Hide not thy face from me, O God, answer me quickly, draw near to my soul, may thy help raise me up.' So there is a darkness present, but through the darkness shines the voice of the prophets and the psalmist. Running all the way through this section is the music 'Hide not thy face from me O God'. It ends very quietly, quite dissonantly, but the dissonance disappears into a single note, at which point comes the apocalyptic voice of God, singing (from the dome): 'I will send you Elijah the prophet, before the great, the terrible day of the Lord.'

Here we arrive at the third part. I repeat, the Fall was once and for all but we have the choice because of the incarnation of the Logos. The doctrine of the God-man refers also and equally to the double nature of the union between God and the whole created world, through man and in man. Hence the introduction at this point of the grand organ in all its magnificence, to mark the incarnation.

Creation is an act which in the eyes of God is above time altogether, since it pertains to the eternal act of the generation of the Logos. Now, again, musically and succinctly, and always remaining close to the metaphysical idea, the ram's-horn trumpet plays its awesome notes which are taken up by all the other brass instruments, producing a tremendous fanfare heralding the incarnation of the Logos. You hear, in Greek, the male voice choir singing objectively, without emotion, the words 'Logos', 'Logos', 'Logos'.

Then chaos begins again, as one hears the voices singing, 'Crucify him! Crucify him! Crucify him!' For the first time we hear a Greek psaltist, singing completely unaccompanied, 'τον σταυρόν σου' – 'Thy cross we adore.' This is repeated, 'Thy cross', 'Thy cross', 'Thy cross'. The ram's-horn trumpet sounds again, the brasses, trumpets, trombones all sound, imitating the ram's-horn rhythm and notes. The music becomes more and more dense, more and more frightening, more and more awesome, as the crucifying begins. The chorus begin to stamp. But then there is a total silence before the moment of Crucifixion itself.

The Crucifixion begins in exactly the same way as the uncreated chaos. It appears to be the same; a return to the thunderous cacophony of uncreated chaos, for the Crucifixion is an unconscious effort by humanity to destroy the divine order. But this anti-God effort fails because it is impossible to destroy the divine.

So the chaos music – which one might be forgiven for thinking was going to go on for yet another five or six minutes – is abruptly cut short after twenty seconds, at which point there are three Hindu temple bowls, pulsing from a great height, and you hear the voice of Mary Magdalene. This should remind the listener of the voice of Eve in Paradise, singing the words 'Ravoni', 'Master', as she falls at the feet of the Risen Christ. This is a moment of ecstasy, as Eve is redeemed, so to speak. This rare, simple recognition of Christ, on a level that is without esotericism – just pure loving – makes it possible for all of us, if we want to, to join in the cosmic dance of the Resurrection. The cosmic dance is the affirmation of all creation and the promise of fulfilment which we cannot see.

Now, the musical notes of the Resurrection are the same notes that appeared in the uncreated chaos, but all the dissonances are removed so everything has become harmonious. Everything is identical – the length of time, the twenty-seven different speeds, the instrumentation – everything is identical except the fact that this is a glorious and harmonious sound, not a terrifying, dissonant, chaotic sound. The very last thing that one hears is the *nāy* (or the *kaval*) indicating the possibility of the return to Paradise at the very end. The *nāy* plays with the double bass (which represents the voice of God throughout), gradually disappearing into silence, the piece ending with another conducted silence of sixty seconds, during which I have instructed (in the case of the St Paul's performance, at least) that all the bells of the cathedral or of the church should be rung.

Fall and Resurrection came to me as a vision. I hope it contains a message of hope for the next millennium. It is divine beauty alone that sets in motion the movement whereby God reveals potentiality in manifest form, so it is the same beauty which rouses in created beings the aspiration for higher existence that is present potentially for all and in all of us.

Fall and Resurrection ideally should be performed in a building with a large acoustic and it should be in the round. The use of the *nāy*, or the *kaval*, and the use of the ram's-horn trumpet and of Tibetan temple gongs is not an act of antiquarianism or exoticism – rather, I would hope that the resonance of these musical instruments would bring to the mind and the soul something primordial, something lost, something innocent, something wild, something untamed. In *Fall and Resurrection* I have tried to compress cosmic events into liturgical time.

Mystagogia

Mystagogia was inspired by a text from *The Divine Names* by St Dionysios the Areopagite:

> We see the Godhead sacredly hymned, on the one hand as a monad and as oneness because of the simplicity and unity of its supernatural undividedness, through which, as a unified force, we are united; the distinctions which divide us are laid aside in a manner surpassing this world, and we are brought together in God-like oneness and union imitating that of God; and on the other hand it is hymned as a Trinity because of the manifestation in three persons with life-giving power which is above all being and from which all lineage in heaven and earth derives its being and its name.

Mystagogia is written in trinitarian guise, hence the use of three small instrumental groups – orchestra one, orchestra two, orchestra three. Orchestra one should be in the middle; the other two groups, which are identical, are on either side, as in the Andrei Rublev ikon of the Trinity. I have attempted in *Mystagogia* to rid myself of the mind and of the emotions and to allow what is left to come through. No one in their right mind wants to hear my music, but rather that of the spirit. Much of the music is secret even to me. It was written quickly – literally without 'thinking'. But to rise in your entirety to the height of holy things, defiled as I am, is dangerous and unobtainable. This kind of writing is always a cross.

May this piece, *Mystagogia*, be accepted therefore as a poor man's mite given to his friends, to the musicians who play it and to all those who hear it.

I looked at the score for the first time since I finished it the other day and felt that I could adore it as something completely beyond me.

Postlude

So it emerges: John Tavener has always composed out of a belief in the presence of another order of reality and, as also emerges, increasingly out of a knowledge that music can rise above the means of its fabrication and act as a channel of communication to that higher reality. It can effectively embody the values and meanings that are entailed by the presence of that reality. This runs counter to many current habits of thought and experience, so it is as well that this Testament should remind us of how deeply mysterious a thing music is.

Tavener's rejection of the accumulated conventions of music-making in recent centuries is certainly radical. But that is doubtless because he begins *before* music, seeing that the nature of music itself points to the necessity of understanding something of the creature for whom it is intended. Among his rejections, no less radical for being less explicit, we should note his view of the human self-image. It is not widely assumed in our post-modern – now post-human – world that man is created in the Divine Image. It emerges from the foregoing Testament that the composer's musical exploration of what constitutes our true humanity is at odds with the contemporary view of man that is more or less vaguely assumed on the basis of a materialist-scientific view of things. Tavener's belief that music is a way to ultimate truths capable of being integrated into life's every moment necessarily hangs upon a religious and metaphysical vision of reality.

Are we not obliged to acknowledge that, integral to such a vision, the composer's view of modernism and all that gave rise to it is the rejection of a type of mentality that persistently denies a higher order of reality? A rejection made in the name of 'the intellective organ of the heart'. In so doing, Tavener draws upon a mode of wisdom that, until the advent of the rationalist Enlightenment, was once taken for granted in the arts. This wisdom had presupposed that truth is not something we are meant to grasp mentally, but something we are called upon to embody in our being. That is to say, our access to truth is not via the more or less cerebral dexterity of reason by which we gather a discursive knowledge of things. Indeed, it is not the scrutiny of existent things that takes us along the path to truth, but an immediate, heartfelt intuition and identity of being beyond mental concepts and thoughts fabricated upon concepts. It is a sharing in and attachment to the living source of things – a direct participation in the one same light and illumination that is the spiritual essence of things. Only the human as such is 'fallen': the intellective organ is that spiritual presence in the heart that pierces our egocentric illusions, the better to illuminate our path to what transcends our 'fallen' nature. It can only flourish to the degree we assent to the divine in us, to the degree we bring our lives and our very being into accord with and contemplate the *logos* within us.

Behind the composer's distinction of the Platonic – a term of approval – from the Aristotelian, the scholastic – a term of censure – is a recognition that the *means* by which music is generated are not in themselves a sufficient reason for musical composition; art is never properly for the sake of art. Tavener's continual effort to transcend the formulae, the procedures, the rules for humanly fabricating music is not a simplistic appeal to abandon discipline, skill and technique in the name of an affected artistic licence. Fabrication here indicates skill deployed in the absence of any contemplative vision, the manipulation of materials not transfigured, and therefore not illuminated, by anything beyond our fallen nature. It is a recognition that true 're-creation' (the term he favours) proceeds according to harmonic laws and consonances shared by heaven and earth.

The ascending 'pull' that is the signature of a truly spiritual music presupposes an economy of means in accordance with the integral needs of that 'intellective organ of the heart'; that is the touchstone of this Testament. It is a movement from the lower faculties of sensation through the intermediate faculties of memory and imagination, to the integrative faculties of intuition and inspiration that finally strikes some reverberation of the eternal reality. An economy of musical resources is necessary in order that both the composer's inspiration and the listener's contemplation do not run riot in too great a diffusion of possibilities. This same economy accounts for the growing simplicity and static pulse of the composer's music, drawing as it does on the sacramental character of the modes of ancient chant.

Herein lies another clue to the composer's motivation in rejecting modernism. The movement from Bach to Mahler saw a continuous expansion in the compositional and instrumental realm of music-making. This development was needed to accommodate the growing emotional vocabulary of music. This vocabulary was itself the result of a growing perception of the autonomy of the subjective world and all it could be made to yield by way of expressing nuances of emotion. It could be said of this development that it was 'natural' in so far as it corresponded to a human impulse, even if it did reflect a growing humanistic narcissism.

The emotional language that eighteenth- and nineteenth-century music so ably embodied collapsed in on itself with the advent of the structural possibilities of instrumental timbre explored, for example, by Debussy, and the breakdown of tonality in the hands of the Second Viennese School of composers. The various 'Orchestral Pieces' of Schoenberg, Berg and Webern, for instance, stand on the threshold of the emotional world of the nineteenth century and the abstraction of the twentieth. From this point forward, music was forcibly obliged to find its aesthetic justification and its compositional resources from within itself. After all, had no less an authoritative voice than that of Stravinsky claimed that music refers to nothing else but itself? Had he not also said that each work obeys certain aesthetic laws that are unique to itself? The qualified validity of this latter idea notwithstanding, a young composer's pushing such a claim to a point of principle can only end in trapping him in the diminishing cycle of innovation and novelty whose sterility must finally engulf him and his audience. The development of atonal and post-atonal music is motivated largely by a technical imperative rather than a human one. The contemporary composer is now all too often the lonely high priest presiding over an ideology of sound ordered almost solely by considerations of technique.

The young John Tavener joined no school, albeit he was certainly heir to this innovatory spirit, only to discover that it did not accord with his essentially religious imagination. He subsequently spent twenty years divesting himself and his music of this legacy. Other voices have summoned him. The spiritual dynamic of the 'intellective organ of the heart' empowers trajectories of joy, sorrow, beauty, love, compassion, awe and reverence, that surmount the limited sphere of egocentric sensibility. At such trajectories the music of John Tavener is aimed.

Chronological List of John Tavener's Compositions

1961
Duo Concertant, for trombone and piano
Portrait d'une Jeune Fille et l'Harpe, for harp, organ, violin
Credo, for tenor solo, chorus, narrator, oboes, brass, organ

1962
Elegy In Memoriam Frank Salisbury, for violin solo and string quartet
Genesis, for tenor solo, chorus, narrator, brass, percussion, organ, piano, string quartet
Piano Concerto (1962–3), for piano solo, horns, timpani, strings
Three Holy Sonnets of John Donne, for baritone solo, brass, percussion, strings

1963
Three sections from T. S. Eliot's Four Quartets, for high voice and piano

1964
The Cappemakers (revised 1965), for narrators, soloists, chorus, orchestra

1965
Cain and Abel, for 4 solo voices and orchestra
The Whale (1965–6), for mezzo and baritone soloists, chorus, narrator, orchestra, tape, men with loud hailers

1967
Grandma's Footsteps, for musical boxes and instrumentalists
Three Surrealist Songs, for mezzo-soprano, tape, piano, bongo drums

1968
Introit for March 27, the Feast of St John Damascene, for soprano and alto soloists, chorus, brass, piano, vibraphone, organ, strings
In Alium, for high soprano solo, Hammond organ, grand organ, piano, strings, tape

1969
Celtic Requiem (1968–9), for high soprano solo, children's chorus, adult chorus, orchestra

1970
Nomine Jesu, for mezzo solo, chorus, 2 alto flutes, chamber organ, 5 male speaking voices
Coplas, for SATB soloists, chorus, tape

1971
Responsorium in Memory of Annon Lee Silver, for 2 mezzo soloists, chorus, flutes
In Memoriam Igor Stravinsky, for 2 alto flutes, chamber organ, handbells

1972
Variations on Three Blind Mice, for orchestra
Ma fin est mon commencement, for chorus, trombones, percussion, cellos
Little Requiem for Father Malachy Lynch, for chorus, flutes, trumpet, organ, strings
Canciones Españolas, for 2 high voices, flutes, organ, harpsichord, percussion
Ultimos Ritos, for mezzo solo, 12 basses, SATB soloists, 5 male speaking voices, chorus, orchestra, tape
Antiphon for Christmas Morning, for soprano voices

1973
Requiem for Father Malachy (revised 1979), for soloists, chorus, orchestra
Thérèse (1973–6), for soprano, bass and 2 tenor soloists, chorus, children's chorus, orchestra

1976
Canticle of the Mother of God, for soprano solo and chorus
The Liturgy of St John Chrysostom, for priest and chorus
Six Russian Folksongs, for soprano solo, domra, chamber ensemble
Palin, for piano solo

1977
A Gentle Spirit, for soprano and tenor soloists, orchestra, tape
Kyklike Kinesis, for soprano and cello soloists, chorus, orchestra
Lamentation, Last Prayer and Exaltation, for soprano solo and handbells

1978
Palintropos, for piano solo and orchestra
The Immurement of Antigone, for soprano solo and orchestra

1979
Greek Interlude, for flute and piano
Six Abbasid Songs, for tenor solo, flutes, percussion
Akhmatova Requiem (1979–80), for soprano and bass soloists, orchestra

1980
Sappho: Lyrical Fragments, for 2 soprano soloists and string orchestra
My Grandfather's Waltz, for piano duet

1981
The Great Canon of St Andrew of Crete, for chorus
Trisagion, for brass quintet
Prayer for the World, for chorus
Mandelion, for organ solo
Risen!, for chorus and orchestra
Funeral Ikos, for chorus

1982
Towards the Son, for 4 bowed psalteries, 3 trebles, orchestra
Doxa, for chorus
The Lord's Prayer, for chorus
Mandoodles, for a young pianist
He Hath Entered the Heven, for trebles with handbells
The Lamb, for chorus

1983
To a Child Dancing in the Wind, for soprano, flute, harp, viola
Sixteen Haiku of Seferis, for soprano and tenor soloists, percussion, strings
Ikon of Light, for chorus and string trio

1984
Little Missenden Calm, for oboe, clarinet, bassoon, horn
Chant, for guitar solo
Mini Song Cycle for Gina, for soprano and piano
Orthodox Vigil Service, for priests, chorus, handbells

1985
Eis Thanaton, for soprano and bass soloists, bass trombones, harp, percussion, strings
Two Hymns to the Mother of God, for chorus
Love Bade Me Welcome, for chorus
Angels, for chorus and organ

1986
Panikhida, for chorus
Akathist of Thanksgiving, for soloists, chorus, percussion, organ, strings
Ikon of St Cuthbert of Lindisfarne, for chorus
In Memory of Cats, for piano solo
Meditation on the Light, for counter-tenor solo, guitar, handbells
Magnificat and Nunc Dimittis, for chorus

1987
The Protecting Veil, for cello solo and string orchestra
The Tyger, for chorus
Prayer (for Szymanowski), for bass solo and piano
Wedding Prayer, for chorus
Many Years, for chorus
The Acclamation, for chorus
God Is With Us, for chorus and organ
Hymn to the Holy Spirit, for three solo trebles plus chorus

1988
Let Not the Prince Be Silent, for double chorus
Ikon of St Seraphim, for baritone and counter-tenor soloists, chorus, orchestra
The Uncreated Eros, for chorus
Apolytikion for St Nicholas, for chorus
The Call, for chorus
Song for Ileana, for flute solo
A Nativity Carol, for girls' chorus
Resurrection, for soloists, chorus, recorders, brass, percussion, organ, string quartet
Ikon of the Crucifixion, for soloists, chorus, brass, percussion, organ, strings

1989
The Hidden Treasure, for string quartet

Lament of the Mother of God, for soprano solo and chorus
Wedding Greeting, for tenor solo and chorus
Eonia, for chorus
Mary of Egypt, for soprano, bass and alto soloists, chorus, children's chorus, orchestra, tape loop
Psalm 121, for chorus
Today the Virgin, for chorus

1990
The Repentant Thief, for clarinet solo, percussion, strings
Thunder Entered Her, for chorus, organ, male voices, handbells
Ikon of the Trinity, for soli soprano and bass plus chorus
We Shall See Him As He Is, for tenor and soprano soloists, chorus, trumpets, percussion, organ, strings
O, Do Not Move, for chorus
A Christmas Round, for chorus
Thrinos, for cello solo

1991
The Apocalypse (1991–2), for tenor, bass, soprano, mezzo and saxophone soloists, 7 male-voice choirs, 7 counter-tenors, children's choir, recorders, brass, percussion, handbells, organ, strings, string quartet
The Last Sleep of the Virgin, for string quartet and handbells
Ikon of the Nativity, for chorus
Let's Begin Again (1991–4), for bass solo, chorus, orchestra, children miming
Eternal Memory, for cello solo and string orchestra
Village Wedding, for chorus

1992
Annunciation, for SATB soloists and chorus
The Child Lived, for soprano and cello
Akhmatova Songs, for soprano and cello
Theophany (1992–3), for orchestra, bandir drum, tape
Hymns of Paradise, for bass solo, boys' voices, 6 violins

1993
The Myrrh Bearer, for viola solo, chorus, percussion
The Lord's Prayer, for chorus
Song for Athene, for chorus
The World Is Burning, for bass solo, chorus, tam-tam

1994
Melina, for soprano solo
Song of the Angel, for soprano and violin soloists, strings
Agraphon, for soprano solo and strings, 2 timpani
Amen, for SATB
Wedding Prayer, for SATB
Innocence, for soprano, tenor, cello and organ soloists, SATB, hand-bells

1995
Tears of the Angels, for violin solo, strings
Prayer to the Holy Trinity, for SATB
Three Antiphons, for SATB
Syvati, for cello solo, SATB
Feast of Feasts, for SSTTB soloists, SATB, 3–4 percussion (2 sets of handbells, tubular bell, large gong, large tam-tam), organ (optional)
Akhmatova Songs, version for soprano and string quartet
Chant, for cello solo
Diódia – String Quartet No. 3
Lament for Phaedra, for cello and soprano

1996
Petra, for singing string ensemble (7 players)
The Hidden Face, for counter-tenor and oboe soloists, 8 violins, 8 violas
Wake Up . . . And Die, for cello solo, orchestral cello section
As One Who Has Slept, for SATB
Hymn of the Unwaning Light, for SATB
Funeral Canticle, for SATB
Notre Père, for children's choir
Out of the Night, for viola solo
Vlepondas, for soprano, baritone and cello

1997
. . . depart in peace . . ., for solo soprano, tampura (optional), strings
Eternity's Sunrise, for soprano solo, flute, oboe, lute, handbells, strings
Apolytikion of St Martin, for SSAATTTBB
Come and Do Your Will in Me, for SATB
Fear and Rejoice, O People, for SATB
The Last Discourse, for soprano, bass and double bass (amplified), soloists, SATB

Lament for Constantinople, for baritone and alto flute
My Gaze Is Ever upon You, for violin, tape
Samaveda, for soprano, flute and tampura
The World, for string quartet and soprano
Fall and Resurrection, for orchestra and soloists
Ypakoë, for piano solo
Voices, for solo soprano, chorus, Tibetan bowls and bells
Zodiacs, for solo piano

1998
Apolytikion of the Incarnation, for SATB
In the Month of Athyr, for narrator plus SATB
Many Years, for the 50th Birthday of HRH The Prince of Wales, for SATB
Prayer for the Healing of the Sick, for SATB
Ravonee, for chorus
Ikon of St Hilda, for chorus
All Ye That in Christ Have Been Baptised, for chorus
Bethel, for chorus
Nipson, for solo counter-tenor plus viol consort

Works in progress
The Fool
The Toll Houses
Zoë
Mystagogia
Total Eclipse
Tribute to Cavafy
The Mother of God
Ιερὸ ὄνειρο
Cries of the Cosmos
Acclamation for the Milennium – 'A New Beginning'
In Memory . . .
The Lord's Prayer
The Heavenly Bridal Chamber

The music of John Tavener is available from Chester Music Ltd, London

Select Discography

A list of currently available recordings, but not including compilation albums containing one or two Tavener works.

Akathist of Thanksgiving
Westminster Abbey Choir, BBC Singers, BBC Symphony Orchestra, Martin Neary
Sony Classical CD SK 64446

Annunciation; Ikon of the Nativity; The Lamb; A Nativity; Today the Virgin; The Lord's Prayer; Many Years; Wedding Prayer; He Hath Entered the Heaven; The Acclamation
Oxford Pro Musica Singers, Michael Smedley
Proudsound PROU CD 136

Eternal Memory
Steven Isserlis: cello, Moscow Virtuosi, Vladimir Spivakov
BMG Classics 09026 619662

Eternity's Sunrise; Song of the Angel; Petra: A Ritual Dream; Sappho: Lyrical Fragments; Funeral Canticle
Patricia Rozario (soprano), Julia Gooding (soprano), George Mosley (baritone), Andrew Manze (violin), Choir and Orchestra of the Academy of Ancient Music, directed by Paul Goodwin
Harmonia Mundi HMU 90 7231

The Great Canon of St Andrew of Crete
The Tallis Scholars directed by Peter Phillips
Gimell/Phillips 454 902 2

Ikon of Light; Funeral Ikos; The Lamb
The Tallis Scholars, Members of the Chilingirian Quartet, Peter Phillips
Gimell/Phillips 454 905 2

Ikon of Light; Two Hymns to the Mother of God; Today the Virgin;
The Tyger; The Lamb; Eonia
The Sixteen, Members of the Duke Quartet, Harry Christophers
Collins Classics CD 14052

Innocence; The Lamb; The Tyger; Annunciation; Two Hymns to the
Mother of God; Little Requiem for Father Malachy Lynch; Song for
Athene
Patricia Rozario (soprano), Graham Titus (bass), Leigh Nixon (tenor),
Alice Neary (cello), English Chamber Orchestra, Westminster Abbey
Choir, Martin Neary
Sony Classical SK 66613

The Lamb; Funeral Ikos; Hymn to the Dormition of the Mother of
God; Hymn to the Mother of God; Magnificat; Nunc Dimittis
Vasari Singers, Jeremy Backhouse
EMI CD EMX 2251

The Last Sleep of the Virgin; The Hidden Treasure
The Chilingirian Quartet with Iain Simcock: handbells
Virgin Classics VC5 45023 2

The Liturgy of St John Chrysostom
The Europa Singers, Clive Wearing
Ikon Records C IKOS 8E

Mary of Egypt
Patricia Rozario, Stephen Varcoe, Chloe Goodchild, Choristers of Ely
Cathedral, Britten-Pears Chamber Choir, Aldeburgh Festival Ensemble
Collins Classics 2CD 70232

Orthodox Vigil Service
Christ Church Cathedral Choir, Francis Grier
Ikon Records IKO 16/17

Panikhida; Ikon of St Cuthbert of Lindisfarne; Apolytikion for St
Nicholas; Funeral Ikos
Voces Angelicae, Ivan Moody
Ikon Records C IKO 21

The Protecting Veil; Thrinos
Steven Isserlis (cello), London Symphony Orchestra, Gennady
Rozhdestvensky
Virgin Classics VC 7 59052-2

The Protecting Veil; Thrinos
Raphael Wallifisch (cello), Royal Philharmonic Orchestra, Justin
Brown
Tring TRP 048

The Protecting Veil; Wake Up . . . and Die
Yo Yo Ma (cello), Baltimore Symphony Orchestra, David Zinman
Sony SK 62821

The Protecting Veil
Josephine Knight (cello), English Sinfonia, Bramwell Tovey
Carlton Classics 30366 01092

The Protecting Veil; In Alium
Maria Kliegel (cello), Eileen Hulse (soprano), Ulster Orchestra, Takuo
Yuasa
Naxos 8 554388

The Protecting Veil; Last Sleep of the Virgin
F. Springuel (cello), I Fiamminghi, R. Werthen
Telarc CD 80487

The Repentant Thief
Andrew Marriner (clarinet), London Symphony Orchestra, Michael
Tilson Thomas
Collins Classics 20052

Svyati; Eternal Memory; Akhmatova Songs; The Hidden Treasure;
Chant
Steven Isserlis (cello), Patricia Rozario (soprano), Kiev Chamber
Choir, Moscow Virtuosi
BMG RCA Red Seal 09026 68761 2

Tears of the Angels; Depart in Peace; My Gaze Is Ever Upon You
Patricia Rozario (soprano), Clio Gould (solo violin), BT Scottish
Ensemble
Linn Records CD CKD 085

Theophany; Eis Thanaton
Bournemouth Symphony Orchestra, City of London Sinfonia, Richard
Hickox, Patricia Rozario (soprano), Stephen Richardson (bass)
Chandos CHAN 9440

*Thunder Entered Her; The Lamb; The Tyger; Two Hymns to the
Mother of God; Responsorium in Memory of Annon Lee Silver; Song
for Athene; Eonia; God Is With Us*
BBC Singers, Christopher Bowers-Broadbent (organ), Simon Joly
Cala CD 88023

*To A Child Dancing in the Wind; Lamentation; Last Prayer and Exal-
tation; Mini Song Cycle for Gina; Melina*
Patricia Rozario, with accompaniment including John Tavener (piano)
Collins Classics CD 14282

*The Uncreated Eros; Magnificat; Nunc Dimittis; The Lamb; Two
Hymns to the Mother of God; Today the Virgin; God Is With Us; Ode
of St Andrew of Crete; Love Bade Me Welcome; The Tyger; Eonia*
Choir of St George's Chapel, Windsor Castle, Christopher Robinson
Hyperion CDA 66464

We Shall See Him As He Is
John Mark Ainsley (tenor), Patricia Rozario (soprano), BBC Welsh
Chorus, The Britten Singers, Chester Festival Chorus, BBC Welsh
Symphony Orchestra, Richard Hickox
Chandos CHAN 9128

The Whale
Anna Reynolds (mezzo), Raimund Herincx (baritone), Alvar Liddell
(speaker), John Tavener (organ and Hammond organ), The London
Sinfonietta and Chorus, David Atherton
Apple CD SAPCOR 15

Index